2 Years to a Million in Real Estate

2 Years to a Million in Real Estate

MATTHEW A. MARTINEZ

McGraw-Hill

New York   Chicago San Francisco Lisbon London
Madrid Mexico City Milan New Delhi San Juan
Seoul Singapore Sydney Toronto

Contents

Acknowledgments

I would like to thank a number of people who made this book possible. The entire team at McGraw-Hill has been absolutely superb to work with. A special debt of gratitude must be extended to Mary Glenn, who believed in this book from the very first day, and also to Karen Schopp, Tama Harris, and Janice Race, whose hard work and dedication made this book a reality.

I thank my real estate mentor, Steve Chaletzky, who has always been extremely generous with his time, words of encouragement, and sage advice. I am also grateful to my trusted and knowledgeable lawyer, Marjorie Adams, who taught me the importance of understanding the laws that govern our industry.

To Dennis Ford, Shawn Neal, Terry Hillery, and Ryan Zahoruiko, my friends and fellow investors, whose enthusiasm and passion for real estate are contagious, and to my childhood friends, Dave, Debbie, Erik, and Greg, who, early in life, set the bar high—thank you. Thanks also to Eric Gerritsen for advising me against returning to the 9-to-5 world and for teaching me, by example, the meaning of patience and perseverance. Lisa, gracias por todo. Para mi, tu eres perfecta. Father Jack, I'm grateful to you for being such a positive role model.

I want to express a special note of gratitude to my siblings, Joey and Becky, who have weathered the storms of life and somehow managed not only to survive but also to thrive and excel. You are a source of great inspiration to me.

And, finally, this book would never have been written without the love and caring of my mother. You taught me that life is not worth living without dreams. Thank you for always believing in me.

Introduction

The way to get started is to stop talking and start doing.

—WALT DISNEY

2 *Years to a Million in Real Estate* presents a true account of the techniques I used to build a multimillion-dollar portfolio of rental apartments, which, with a bit of good fortune and considerable hard work, allowed me to replace the salary from my job with the rental income from my tenants. It is an accurate journal of my transformation from a financially dependent executive at a high-tech company to a financially independent real estate entrepreneur. Using this book, you'll gain a unique insight into my personal struggle to gain more control of my future. It also reveals precisely how I accomplished the dream of leaving my day job through the acquisition of income-producing properties. More important, it will teach you how to duplicate my achievements, should you choose a similar path for yourself.

According to the Society for Human Resource Professionals:

- 83 percent of all employees plan to seek a new job when the economy improves.
- 35 percent of "top-performing" employees say that they will leave when they can.
- 60 percent of employees feel too much pressure to work.
- 83 percent want more time with their families.
- 56 percent are dissatisfied with their jobs.

Introduction

A CNN/Money article declared: "Overworked employees are fed up: A survey finds 8 out of 10 Americans want something new!"

Like most others in the traditional job pool, I have experienced similar feelings of resentment at being overworked and underpaid. I also experienced a great deal of job anxiety caused by the fear of being laid off during poor economic times or during the inevitable corporate "restructurings" that seem to occur every few years. In fact, when the dot-com bubble burst in 2001, I was gainfully employed by one of those high-flying Internet juggernauts. As the company began dismissing employees, I found myself agonizing over the prospect of being let go before I had secured another source of income to substitute for the paycheck I had grown accustomed to receiving.

The Internet boom of the late 1990s was something that I gratefully benefited from and thoroughly enjoyed. I would certainly not trade those years for anything. Traveling the world with an unlimited budget, working 20-hour days with boundless energy and enthusiasm, and receiving ample stock options—life couldn't have been better during the Internet's gilded age!

Then, suddenly, it all came to an end. After Alan Greenspan, the chairman of the Federal Reserve, uttered the now infamous words "irrational exuberance," profitability became the only thing that mattered to dot-com companies that wanted to survive. The liberal and carefree funding of anything with a ".com" attached to it had dried up. Being forced to pull ourselves away from the money hydrant made us realize just how good it had really been. Now, if you weren't a profitable company or at least on the road to near-term profitability, you were about to become obsolete.

At the time, I had been working as the director of international business development for Lycos (www.lycos.com). It was one of the top five search engines in the world and certainly the most successful portal on the East Coast. My boss's stock options provided him with ample funds to maintain his family's standard of living, so he announced his imminent departure. Fortunately, for him, he was leaving on his own terms (when, where, and how). I, too, wanted to plan my own exit. Every two months, Lycos dismissed another 50 to 100 people. In fact, the first series of layoffs took place while I was working in Sydney planning the launch of our Australian operations. My colleagues in Boston informed me that those who were let go weren't even given the decency of being notified of their fate. Rather, they were blindsided and quickly dismissed by their managers. They had 15 minutes to place their personal belongings in boxes and were humiliatingly escorted out of the building. Apparently, it was a miserable experience for all involved.

When I returned from Australia, the downsizing continued, slowly but ever so methodically. Although I was well respected and had contributed significantly to my company's international expansion and early success, I suspected that my name was on the HR department's hit list. I felt entirely helpless, yet I refused to accept the idea that someone else could dictate my fate, economic well-being, and financial security.

My most immediate concerns were:

- What type of severance package could I negotiate should I be dismissed?
- How long does unemployment insurance last?
- How quickly could I find a job in this depressed employment market?
- How much does health insurance cost?
- Where did I save the latest version of my résumé?

Although I had been compensated handsomely during those years and had never spent beyond my means, I was accustomed to my monthly paycheck. I couldn't stop thinking about becoming just another employment statistic at the U.S. Department of Labor.

With what I had learned from real estate books, of which I had been a voracious reader since my early twenties, coupled with the formal knowledge I had gained from the numerous real estate classes I had taken in college and the fear of being laid off, I quickly came to the conclusion that it was time for me to pursue the vast possibilities afforded to those who own income-producing real estate. It was time to take more control of my life, rather than wait for the vice president of human resources to eventually call me into his office.

More often than not, the need to survive serves as a catalyst for accomplishing great and extraordinary feats in one's life. Fortunately, I had always agreed with Alexander Graham Bell's declaration: "When one door [of opportunity] closes another door opens." You just have to be courageous enough to realize that change is inevitable and that you must pursue your dreams with steadfast conviction and resolve.

In an effort to establish some sort of financial security and as a hedge against corporate downsizing, I began acquiring rental properties. Admittedly, I was terrified by the idea of increasing my debt exposure during a period of economic uncertainty. Fortunately, however, after just two years, the income generated from my rentals exceeded my salary. My part-time "gig" as a landlord quickly became my full-time vocational passion, one that provides me with sufficient income that I'll never have to depend on another employer for my financial security. The exhilaration and sense of freedom I experience from being a self-employed real estate investor have exceeded my wildest expectations.

More millionaires have made their fortunes in real estate than in any other business. In fact, the IRS has reported that 71 percent of all Americans declaring $1 million or more on their income tax returns during the past 50 years were in real estate or related activities. Indeed, real estate can be extremely lucrative and has proved to be the most statistically likely way to achieve financial independence. Income-producing properties (when acquired and managed properly) can generate more income and offer greater flexibility and security than most traditional jobs. You can leave your day job confidently if you are willing to work long hours, demonstrate your tenacity for succeeding, and simply persevere. And, I will show you how I did it in less than two years with rental properties.

1

Why Real Estate Is Better Than 9-to-5!

*You see that building over there? I bought it three
years ago. It was my first real estate transaction. I
sold it 10 months later and made $800,000 profit. It
was better than sex. At the time it was all the money
in the world. Now, it's a day's pay.*
—GORDON GEKKO, FROM THE MOVIE *WALL STREET*

Upon reading that 80 percent of self-made millionaires made their
fortunes by owning real estate, I decided that this industry was my
ticket to an extraordinary life.

In 2002, I had been working in the high-tech industry for 10 years,
and I realized that I wasn't getting any richer, although I was certainly
working many hours. I knew there had to be a better way. I wanted to
earn more, gain more financial security, and have more time for travel,
hobbies, family, friends, and myself. The need to have greater control of
my life was insatiable. Working long hours had never been the problem;

however, I preferred to work diligently while profiting handsomely from my own blood, toil, tears, and sweat, as Mr. Churchill once said.

After graduating from college at age 21, I accepted a position with Shell Oil Company in Los Angeles. I was making $34,000 in 1991 and living paycheck to paycheck while I paid down my student loans. After attending graduate school, I was making $50,000 working for a high-tech company in Washington, D.C., and still my net worth was negligible. In 1997 (two years later), I was working in Arizona making $75,000 and had a net worth of about $50,000 (mostly in 401(k) and IRA accounts). In 1999, I was living in Boston earning more than $100,000, but still my net worth had increased only marginally.

My parsimonious spending habits didn't permit much extravagance, nor did my financial upbringing lend itself to keeping up with the Joneses. Nevertheless, it was nearly impossible for me to develop any significant and meaningful wealth after paying all of my expenses. In other words, I never spent more than I earned, nor did I have poor spending habits, but I just couldn't amass any significant amount of wealth. Although my salary increased every year, my actual net worth amounted to very little. It was all too obvious that my dream of becoming financially independent before age 35 would be increasingly more difficult if I continued to follow the same career path.

I realized that trading hours for dollars was a grave mistake. Working long and hard in corporate America rarely allows one to attain financial security. Yet, I had always been taught in school that I should study hard, earn my degree, and find a high-paying job. (Robert Kiyosaki of *Rich Dad, Poor Dad* fame speaks of this in several of his books and claims that these teachings are a principal defect inherent in our school systems.) This philosophy lends itself to a lifetime of financial dependence, vocational insecurity, and years of laboring only to make someone else wealthy. They just don't teach you how to make money and build significant net worth in college!

Karl Marx wrote in *Das Kapital* that an employer can't possibly pay you what you're worth because a company's profit is the difference between your salary and your actual value. If a company paid all of its employees what they're worth, it would never make a profit and would eventually go out of business. Therefore, as I see it, you have two choices in life: You can choose to be your own boss, or you can choose to allow a company to exploit your true value. Understanding the socialist perspective on capitalism enabled me to confront this problem with great resolve.

Economic wealth provides you with the freedom to choose the lifestyle you want to pursue. After you secure the basic human needs of shelter, food, and housing, you'll have the opportunity to pursue more noble goals only when you have the money to do it. If you have the financial resources, it's really up to you how you spend your time.

This book emphasizes the achievement of a particular lifestyle—not just wealth, but to excel at a satisfying career, to start your own business, to be your own boss, to establish yourself in a dynamic industry, to maintain or advance your standard of living, and to spend more time with the people you love. You will not learn how to become the next Donald Trump, nor will you read the words "billionaire real estate investor" in the following chapters. Instead, you'll simply learn how to replace your salary with the income generated from your real estate holdings so that you can have the opportunity to leave your day job without the fear of financial ruin. Rather than becoming a corporate workaholic in today's stressful society of downsizing and economic insecurity, you will be able to control your own destiny and build a bright financial future on your own terms.

Roosevelt, Field, and Carnegie were bullish on real estate as well:

Real estate is the basis for all wealth.

—THEODORE ROOSEVELT

Buying real estate is the best, safest way to become wealthy.

—MARSHALL FIELD

80 percent of all millionaires made it through real estate.

—ANDREW CARNEGIE

Why Invest in Real Estate?

Only 5 percent of North Americans are financially independent when they reach retirement age. The rest (or a staggering 95 percent) are dependent on family, friends, religious organizations, and charities to make ends meet. If you envision a comfortable lifestyle during retirement with the proceeds from your social security checks but don't manage to save a good portion of your income before retirement, you'll definitely need another plan. If you expect your social security checks to maintain your lifestyle later in life, you are going to have to either continue working well past retirement age or have an extremely meager lifestyle until your eventual death. In my opinion, you should forget about social security. Generation X and the echo boomers will probably never see these funds. I certainly don't count on social security, nor do I lose sleep over what's being done about it on Capitol Hill. You can't depend on social security or any other government program to support you during retirement. Being dependent on anyone other than yourself is a major miscalculation. A prudent plan to safeguard your retirement is to acquire income-producing properties while you are relatively young and pay them off over the course of time so that you can live off the rental revenue stream when you are too old to work. A more aggressive plan would be to buy rental properties and continue to leverage them until you have amassed a sizeable portfolio with a cash flow that can sustain your lifestyle through retirement.

Your savings have less buying power every year because of the effects of inflation. Investing in assets that not only provide a good return but also appreciate in value at a rate significantly above the rate of inflation is paramount for a sound retirement plan. Not only does real estate achieve these goals, but you also receive the added benefit of tax advantages. The deductibility of depreciation, operating expenses, property taxes, and mortgage interest, along with 1031 tax exchange laws, makes real estate the investment of choice when one considers all of its economic advantages.

The most successful investors I know have been in the real estate business for quite a long time and have paid their dues in the early days by responding to irate tenants, clogged toilets, broken windows, and other commonplace but critical maintenance issues. Afterward, they upgraded the size and location of their properties and were able to hire a property manager to deal with the day-to-day headaches. Realizing that they can make more money by using their brains than by using their brawn, they now manage the managers and spend more time looking for new deals while eliminating the unpleasant and time-consuming contact they once had with their tenants.

Eventually, the investors who maintained a small portfolio of properties were able to pay off their mortgages and thus eliminate the vast majority of their annual expenses. At that point, the properties begin to generate significant cash flow. The investors who opted to grow their holdings substantially, as opposed to paying off the mortgages, continued to leverage their holdings to acquire more income-producing properties with even greater overall cash flow. They actually increased their debt by refinancing or extracting equity to finance more acquisitions. You can only decide how large you want to grow your business and how much responsibility (10 tenants versus 1,000) you care to assume. Either way, making money in real estate requires patience, dedication, and perseverance, but the rewards are well worth the time invested.

The revenue generated by your income-producing properties will enable you to earn more money than you do by working for someone else. When you make the transition from part-time landlord to full-time investor, you'll be able to dedicate all of your resources to maintaining or expanding your real estate empire.

The financial and personal benefits of real estate investing are numerous.

Appreciation

Real estate values have experienced a steady increase in value for the last several years. This appreciation is due to the overwhelming demand for real estate. Besides serving as a basic human need (shelter) that everyone on the planet must satisfy, several other factors are working to increase the demand for real estate. For instance, the vast majority of baby boomers (the 85 million Americans born between 1946 and 1964) are approaching their retirement age and are buying, in record numbers, second homes—condos in the city or vacation properties in the mountains or near the ocean. The echo boomers (78 million in total—the children of the baby boomers) have just begun to buy their first homes and rent their first apartments. Immigration accounts for approximately 1.2 million new inhabitants of our country each year and will continue to do so for the foreseeable future. Immigrants (especially Hispanics) tend to have more children (i.e., a higher birth rate) than native-born Americans; thus, our country's population will continue to increase from within. In fact, the estimated population of the United States by 2050 is 420 million. That's a staggering 42 percent increase, while Europe's population will decline by 10 percent and Japan's by 21 percent during the same period. If the U.S. population continues to expand at these rates, the demand for available housing will, logically, increase as well. The divorce rate has passed 50 percent, forcing both parents to buy homes instead of living in a single property. People are living longer (70, 80, and 90 years of age is not uncommon), and the elderly will continue to apply additional pressure on the current housing stock. All of these factors will continue to create significant demand in the housing market during the coming years.

Leverage

Leverage is the use of borrowed funds to finance the purchase of an asset. Leverage allows you to use other people's money (often referred to as OPM) to buy more properties, and real estate investors use leverage to increase their purchasing power and finance investments that they cannot pay for otherwise. Leverage also allows investors to earn a higher return on their equity. For example, leverage allows you to buy a $1 million property with only $200,000. How else could you buy a million-dollar asset for 20 percent down? In fact, you can buy most properties for much less. If the property appreciates in value by 10 percent in the first year, it will be worth $1,100,000. If you don't use leverage (you buy the property in cash), your return on equity is 10 percent. If you use leverage (say 20 percent down or $200,000), then your return on equity is not 10 percent but 50 percent ($100,000/$200,000). You'd be hard-pressed to generate a return of this magnitude by investing in mutual funds.

You can extract money from the existing value (the equity) of your properties and use it as a down payment to acquire more rental units. When I first began investing in real estate, I couldn't imagine how investors saved 20 percent of the purchase price for a typical $400,000 property. How was it possible to save $80,000? Ask any successful investor if he managed to sock away the requisite funds for a down payment by working 9-to-5, and he'll probably tell you that he leveraged his existing home or income-producing properties to buy more properties.

I happened to leverage the equity in my primary residence to acquire my first investment property. I doubt that most people would be able to save $80,000 from their day job for the down payment—forget about it!

Successful real estate investors use as little of their own capital as possible to acquire as much property as possible. Keep your hard-earned money for emergencies, and use the bank's money to finance new acquisitions.

Very few, if any, investment vehicles compare to real estate in terms of cash-on-cash return. Real estate allows you to leverage your current holdings to take possession of extremely valuable assets. Leverage is the key ingredient that makes real estate the most profitable of investment choices.

With $40,000, you could buy a $400,000 property using an 80 percent first loan for $320,000, a 10 percent second loan (often referred to as a piggyback loan) for $40,000 and your own 10 percent down payment. The $40,000 down payment might come from the equity you have in your primary residence or another investment property, thus making this a zero-down acquisition. You never had to use your savings to buy this $400,000 asset! In many cases, you can find an aggressive bank or lender that will provide you with even better terms. (Financing terms are a bit more strict for commercial properties—buildings with five or more apartments.) If the property appreciates by 10 percent each year for three years, it will then be worth $532,400. You have increased your net worth by $132,400 in only 36 months. Try duplicating these results by contributing to your company's 401(k) program—it will never happen.

You must remember this one key strategy to secure your financial success in the early days of your investing career: there is good debt, and there is bad debt. Knowing the difference is absolutely critical. Good debt is used to buy real estate and other assets that tend to appreciate and make money over time. Bad debt is used to acquire liabilities such as cars and boats. These items are very nice to have and make you feel good, but they also immediately lose value and do not appreciate over time. Use debt wisely to buy more of the former and less of the latter.

Tax Savings

If you acquire the right properties at a good price and manage them well, your rental properties will generate a positive cash flow, but because of substantial tax write-offs (including depreciation), they might show a paper loss for tax purposes. Thus, you are not obligated to pay taxes on your gains. Let's say a property generates $1,000 a month in positive before-tax cash flow (cash flow before taxes = gross operating income less operating expenses, debt service, and capital additions). You would pocket $12,000 a year. Well, let's assume the depreciation amounted to $15,000 for the same period. Not only would you show a $3,000 paper loss, you'd actually avoid having to pay taxes on the $12,000 gain for that year.

Imagine having four or five of these moneymaking machines and not having to pay taxes (or paying a marginal tax) on the gains . . . sheer bliss, right? Moreover, if you buy your primary residence and sell the property after living in it for two years (two of the past five years, to be exact), you'll pay absolutely no capital gains taxes on your first $250,000 profit if you're single, and no capital gain taxes on the first $500,000 if you're married. You can use part of these funds to buy another home and the remaining funds to buy more rental properties. There's no better tax incentive. That said, you might want to consider moving every two years.

Cash Flow

A common strategy of many investors is to create a steady stream of cash from each property, as if each building were a separate and distinct business. The initial goal is to create enough sources of revenue so that the total they provide can eventually replace your paycheck. Many investors, including myself, actually live off the income streams from their properties, and the income can be quite significant if you purchased the properties at a discount or if the mortgages are paid off. Cash flow is defined as the amount obtained when annual debt service (mortgages) and capital improvements are subtracted from the net operating income. Stated more simply, it's the amount of money you have leftover after all the bills are paid.

Your tenants pay your mortgages, thus creating an enormous amount of equity in your properties over the course of time. Eventually, they will pay off the mortgages completely, and you'll own the rental units free and clear. Your buildings will appreciate, and your net worth will soar. The positive cash flow you'll receive each month will provide you with a healthy income, so you won't feel obligated to work a traditional job just to survive. Becoming financially independent is statistically more likely in this business than in any other.

Reliability

Since the beginning of time, real estate has been recognized as one of the most reliable assets to own. It is easy to borrow against, should you need extra capital, because banks are willing to lend you money if the loan is secured by property. Real estate is fundamentally sound because everyone needs a roof over his head, and it is always in demand because of its basic and fundamental utility. Individuals have been investing in real estate long before there was a stock, bond, or commodity market.

Freedom from a 9-to-5 Job

Although some management and record keeping are required, your time commitment can be minimal compared to that required by most other businesses. If you invested in a software company, consulting firm, coffee shop, or bakery, you would be married to the business, and you would have to dedicate many long hours to its success. Real estate investing can be done (at least before you create an expansive empire) without too much interference with your current job. It doesn't require your attention 24 hours a day. Once the apartments are rented, you simply need to field phone calls from the tenants when their units require maintenance. You can dispatch a plumber, electrician, or carpenter with a quick phone call from the convenience of your home or office. The nature of this business allows you to maintain your salaried position while growing your new source of revenue. Once you've replaced your salary with sufficient rental income, you'll then be in the enviable position of being able to devote all your time to your rental business.

My properties continue to make money for me, regardless of whether I'm physically there or not. That said, I'm certainly not advocating that you become an absentee landlord or that you neglect your properties; however, you don't need to spend 10 hours a day at your properties watching the grass grow (as is expected at most traditional day jobs). Once you've dealt with the major issues, your properties should operate smoothly (assuming that you did your homework, selected your tenants carefully, and addressed all major property concerns—see the chapters on selecting tenants and property management). For long periods of time I don't receive a single call from my tenants. I typically spend February in Florida, and I can manage my properties with a cell phone and laptop. Admittedly, there are other months when I do receive several phone calls, and there can be a significant amount of work required to properly manage both tenant- and building-related issues. In the beginning, I visited my properties every two weeks, regardless of whether they required any work. I've concluded that if my tenants think I'm never checking on them, they might do something they shouldn't. Sometimes only the paranoid can survive in this business. Whether it's a busy month or a carefree month, real estate offers a much more flexible lifestyle than any other line of work that I'm aware of.

I feel the need to advise new investors that, once you own a certain number of units, you'll start to feel the pressure of both managing your portfolio of properties and working at your day job. I was able to manage both for several years. Everyone has a limit to the aggravation and stress he can endure, however, so be aware of what your own threshold is and learn to manage your time as best you can.

About 99 percent of self-made millionaires come from these four categories:

- Self-owned businesses (74 percent)
- Senior executive positions (10 percent)
- Doctors, lawyers, and other professionals (10 percent)
- Salespeople or sales consultants (5 percent)

The final 1 percent percent of self-made millionaires consists of people in all other areas—inventors, actors, athletes, and authors.

If you want to be financially independent and you have an appreciation of entrepreneurship, then you should try to start your own business. Real estate just happens to be one very good option in which the odds of generating significant wealth are actually in your favor.

Once you understand the major advantages of investing in real estate, it is easy to conclude that very few, if any, other investments can match it. It is the principal means of wealth accumulation for financially independent individuals.

2

How I Did It: Primary Residence–Condo

The only thing that separates successful people from the ones who aren't is the willingness to work very, very hard.

—Helen Gurley Brown

January 2000

Although I don't generally recommend buying a single condominium for cash flow purposes, I bought one as my primary residence, and fortunately, it turned out to be a wise investment. At the time, I didn't know any better, and I wasn't buying the condo with a long-term investment or rental strategy in mind. Instead, I was buying it to put a roof over my head while I worked at my day job.

As an income property, the rent generated from a single condo typically does not pay all the costs to maintain the property. In other words, the rent will not pay the mortgage, taxes, and monthly maintenance fee.

Condos tend to have a negative cash flow or, at best, to provide a break-even scenario (you don't earn money, but you don't lose money). You must avoid properties with negative cash flow, where you are paying out of your own pocket to maintain a property. Furthermore, investments that don't sustain themselves based on fair market rents are simply not good investment choices. It is true that significant profit has been made through appreciation alone; however, you must not count on appreciation for future gains. Appreciation is an ancillary benefit of ownership, whereas a positive cash flow is a prerequisite. Investors who can distinguish between the two tend to be substantially more successful over the long term.

If I had understood (as I do now) the dynamics of real estate at that time, I would have acquired a three- or four-family building and lived in one of the units, allowing my tenants to pay the full mortgage. Although the initial purchase price and operating expenses are substantially greater for a multiunit property, the subsequent risk and ongoing expenses are typically less relative to the revenue generated by the rentals. Moreover, if you buy a small apartment building as your primary residence and live in one of the apartments and rent the others, you can qualify for lower interest rates than if you were to acquire the building as a nonowner-occupant investment property.

I purchased my first condo for $200,000 in 1999. All of my friends thought I had paid a premium for the property and even questioned my sanity. Fortunately, I acquired the condo, which was in a neighborhood experiencing tremendous appreciation, at an opportune time. Although the economy began its downward descent in 2000, home appreciation, and especially condo values in the Northeast (and most other parts of the country, as well), by contrast, reached new heights. It was ultimately the appreciation on this one condo that provided me with the means to buy my first few income-producing properties. In fact, most of the individuals who had purchased units in the same building were cashing out of their places and upgrading their homes with the gains. They were living more luxurious lifestyles, and paying for those lifestyles with the appreciation gained during the previous two years. I, however, decided to maintain the same relatively simple lifestyle and invest the equity in assets that would not only make me more money in the future, but also generate positive cash flows and appreciate over time. Instead of buying a larger home and having to pay a significantly larger mortgage, I opted to live in the same place and buy a rental property. I was confident that this strategy would eventually pay off and that someday I'd be able to buy a larger home, but for now, I'd simply have to sacrifice for a few more years.

After living in the condo for two years, I received a call from the real estate broker who helped me find the unit. He asked if I'd be interested in meeting with another one of his clients, who was interested in acquiring the unit beneath mine for use as his office. I agreed, and a few days later I had lunch with the prospective buyer. Fortunately, this individual happened to be a third-generation real estate investor with significant holdings in the area, so I expressed my intention of buying income-producing properties. He was supportive of my endeavor and encouraged me to contact him should I have any questions. During the months and years that followed, he received numerous phone calls and e-mails from me and he graciously fielded all of my inquiries. He became my mentor and voice of reason as I began acquiring apartment buildings. He not only reviewed my property analysis worksheets but he also introduced me to plumbers, roofers, electricians, and other vendors who helped me manage my properties. More important, these vendors returned my phone calls and performed high-quality work at a reasonable price. Everyone needs a mentor, and I suggest that you find someone who can help you, too.

Being a landlord is not as easy as it seems. It's a complex business that requires mastery of human psychology, mathematical modeling, and micro- and macroeconomics, and, at times, even some knowledge of structural engineering. Knowing a bit about plumbing, electric wiring, and carpentry doesn't hurt, either. At the end of the day, it's a business, and your clients are people. You manage your properties, but you service your tenants. And, you must know how to do both very well. If you have 12 individuals living in four buildings, then you'll have 12 different personalities and four structures that differ in a multitude of ways. Learning the best ways to manage both is paramount to your success.

Lessons Learned

- Don't buy a condo for cash flow. You might buy one as a primary residence or a vacation home, but it's unlikely that you'll generate enough income to pay all the carrying costs associated with the property. Never buy a negative cash flow property.
- If you acquire a condo strictly for rental purposes, it's likely that you'll have to pay out-of-pocket each month to carry the unit, unless, of course, you buy at an extraordinarily low price or buy the property without obtaining a mortgage (an all-cash purchase).
- If you're losing money each month, the only way you'll make a profit is if the property appreciates in value and you sell it for a gain. This is not a wise strategy to pursue, although many investors and speculators have made money doing it. Betting on appreciation is extremely dangerous, especially if you catch a real estate cycle headed in the wrong direction.
- If a condo is the only property you can afford and you're buying it as a primary residence, then do what I did and withdraw the equity (assuming that the condo does appreciate) to buy larger investment properties that generate a positive cash flow.
- Find a real estate mentor. You'll benefit immensely from a knowledgeable and experienced person who has been where you want to go.

3

First Income-Producing Property

The difference between a successful person and others is not a lack of strength, not a lack of knowledge, but rather a lack of will.

—VINCE LOMBARDI

June 2002

As I mentioned in the Introduction, in February 2002, my boss left Lycos, and I knew that it was just a matter of time before I either left of my own accord or fell victim to the downsizing that was taking place. With that in mind, I set my sights on a part of Boston that met my acquisition criteria and determined that now was the time for me to start investing. My strategy included the following:

- Buy properties within a 30-minute drive from my own home.
- Locate properties in an up-and-coming neighborhood that showed great promise for improving over time.

- Find properties that were near public transportation (subways and bus routes) and close to the principal job centers (downtown).
- Acquire properties that generated a positive cash flow even with a modest (0 to 10 percent) down payment.
- Close on properties that were situated in neighborhoods that I felt comfortable and safe visiting on a regular basis.

With these parameters in mind, I chose a neighborhood that was still undervalued, yet had great potential for growth because of its proximity to the downtown area as well as the gentrification that had taken place in adjacent towns. It was just a matter of time before my targeted area would improve as well.

After selecting a specific location, it was then necessary for me to decide which part of that town was the optimal place in which to invest. Even within a small neighborhood, there are good and bad areas. Real estate is incredibly local, so you need to familiarize yourself with every nook and cranny of your target location. One street north of Main Street might be infested with crime, while two streets south of it might be an ideal location to own. Don't be in a rush to buy if you don't know the area in which you are investing. Be sure to take your time, and by all means do your homework.

Once I had decided where to buy, I needed a strategy for finding the right properties. I visited all the major real estate brokerage firms that specialized in apartment buildings and asked to speak with the most successful agents at each office. I define "successful" as the brokers who sold the most property and had the most listings (in dollar terms) during the past three to five years. If you simply show up at a Realtor's office, you'll be forced to work with the agent who is working the floor at the time you show up. That sales agent might have only two months of experience and is unlikely to serve your needs. Because you're looking for a very specific type of property and relying on your agent to provide you with detailed market information and local expertise, I always opt for experienced agents over inexperienced ones even if they demonstrate a tremendous amount of energy and enthusiasm.

I drove around the target neighborhood looking at FSBO (for sale by owner) opportunities, as well as buildings that weren't even on the market. If I saw a property that met my criteria, I would simply knock on the door and ask to speak with the owner. Many times, the owner didn't live in the property, so the tenants would provide me with the owner's or property manager's contact information. I called a number of them inquiring about their interest in selling their properties. I also scoured the real estate section of local newspapers, searching for new properties, and I toured all the multifamily open houses each Sunday. In the meantime, I obtained a preapproval letter from a local bank and established banking relationships with several other financial institutions. I interviewed potential lenders and created a spreadsheet of more than 50 mortgage brokers and lending institutions, detailing their terms, rates, and lending programs. This spreadsheet allowed me to compare and contrast their programs. By understanding all of my financing options, I would be able to select the most competitive lender when the time came.

Having worked in the high-tech industry for nearly a decade, I was accustomed to creating business plans for newly proposed projects. After doing my homework and determining a strategy, I decided to put it all down on paper, so I created an 80-plus-page prospectus. This helped me to better analyze the opportunity and consider all the strengths and weaknesses in my proposed plan. In fact, I originally wanted to find investors to finance the acquisition of the properties instead of using my own capital. I pitched my business plan to everyone I knew who had sufficient financial resources, and I was rejected by each and every one of them. After spending three months in a failed attempt to raise $1 million, I opted to put my money (aka the equity in my home) where my mouth was and used my own capital to execute the plan I had outlined.

One day in April 2002, when I was at work, I received a call from a real estate broker who had placed me on her investor contact list after I had repeatedly pestered her to send me worthwhile opportunities. When they initially receive a listing, and before putting it on the MLS (Multiple Listing Service), many real estate agents contact their best customers to broker a quick sale. This is referred to as a pocket listing. Agents may retain the full commission (typically ranging from 5 to 6 percent of the sales price) if they both list the property for sale and find the buyer. They won't have to share their commission (forfeit 2 to 3 percent of the sales price) with anyone else (i.e., the buyer's broker) if they work both ends of the deal. Another advantage is that the listing agent is able to secure a quick sale to an experienced investor who won't be likely to default on the deal because of their lack of experience, inability to secure financing, or fear of the unknown.

This broker informed me that she had just received a listing that met my criteria, and that she would allow me to view the property (a three-unit apartment building) before listing it on MLS the next day. I immediately left work and drove to the building for a quick tour. Within 15 minutes, I knew that this was the one. I decided to make an offer based on a 15 percent reduction of the asking price that would expire within 24 hours if not accepted. The seller and I settled on a price and a closing date, and the real estate broker never had to list the property or attend any open houses. Nevertheless, she was paid a 5 percent commission, and both the seller and I were pleased with the results.

Now that my offer had been accepted, I needed money for the down payment to close on my first investment property. Fortunately, my primary residence (the condo) had appreciated significantly, allowing me to extract the requisite funds in the form of a cash-out refinancing. By refinancing from a 30-year fixed-rate mortgage to a five-year adjustable with a larger principal balance, yet at a substantially lower rate, I was actually able to maintain a similar monthly mortgage payment. I used the proceeds from my refinancing to buy my first investment property (applying 20 percent down at closing) during the summer of 2002. This is when it all began.

This transaction was a bit complicated because the owner was living on the third floor and was moving out after the sale. The owner's tenants had been occupying the first and second floors for the past 15 or 20 years and were paying only a fraction of the fair market rent. The owner had agreed in writing to sell the house completely vacant. Unfortunately, both tenants were noncommittal and hadn't found a new apartment by the closing date, and they were unable to pay current market rents. I was given an ultimatum: buy the property with the two existing tenants who were paying about 30 percent of what they should be paying, or back out of the deal. I opted to buy the property with a few conditions.

Before the closing, my lawyer and I convinced the seller to escrow six months of rent (the difference between the market rent and the rent currently being paid) to compensate me for any losses incurred after the purchase. If the tenants moved out earlier, the seller would receive the amount of the funds that remained. The owner was told to serve a no-fault eviction notice to the tenants so as to expedite the process. The seller agreed to my requests, and the sale went through as planned.

Never let a good opportunity die. Creativity is an essential skill in this industry, and you need think unconventionally to shepherd challenging deals to the closing table.

The tenants eventually found new housing five months later, but I was able to use almost all of the escrowed funds to pay for the discrepancy in the rental income. After the tenants left, I quickly renovated the units and rented them out at market rates.

The original tenants were far better off because they had been living in apartments that were outdated. And, my new tenants were better off because they moved into newly renovated and modernized living quarters. I benefited because I generated enough rental income to pay the mortgage and operating expenses while earning a very nice monthly profit.

Lessons Learned

- Select a target area in which to buy your investment properties. Determine your property criteria and do your homework so that you fully understand the pros and cons of each location.
- Act quickly if you can acquire a good deal. Time is always of the essence.
- Work with creative and experienced attorneys who are able to suggest and implement solutions that will help you achieve your goals.
- If you buy a property under unusual circumstances or are aware of repairs that are needed, then you should ask the seller for some sort of financial compensation. Don't demand that the seller make the repairs himself, because it's likely that he'll do it without the attention to detail that you would apply. Instead, determine a fair price for all the repairs and negotiate a discount on the sale of the property.

- Be creative with how you structure the acquisition. The objective is to reduce your overall risk and initial expense with any new property acquisition while maintaining a positive cash flow each month.

Date: June 2002

Total rental units: 3
Value of rental properties: $390,000

4

Second Income-Producing Property

You can tell a man is clever by his answers. You can tell a man is wise by his questions.

—Naguib Mahfouz

After such a positive experience with my first building, I decided to double up and try my luck with another one. If I could generate as much positive cash flow with my next building as I had with my first, I'd be in an enviable financial position and one step closer to leaving my day job. My condo (as mentioned in the last chapter) had appreciated to $365,000 (providing me with $165,000 in equity), so I was able to draw more equity from the property to acquire my second apartment building.

I spent weeks driving around my target neighborhood searching for my next great deal. Then, suddenly, I stumbled across a brand-new three-family building.

This property had originally been developed as a condo conversion project; however, the owner was in the midst of buying a very large apartment complex in Pittsburgh and needed the cash to close that deal. Therefore, she couldn't wait to sell three individual units and opted for a quick exit (albeit with less profit) by selling the entire building at once.

After spending an hour with the listing broker, I was able to determine the following:

1. The seller was motivated to make a quick sale because she needed the funds to make the Pittsburgh purchase.
2. The building was condo-ready, so each of the units was separately metered for utilities and in excellent condition.
3. The building had just been completed and, thus, was brand-new construction built to the latest code. There had been a fire on the premises two years earlier, so the new owner had rebuilt the structure from the foundation up. With a new frame, insulation, windows, roof, heating systems, electric wiring, and plumbing, the maintenance costs would be significantly less than those of an older building of the same size.
4. The property had already been under agreement; however, the buyer's financing had fallen through at the last moment. The building had returned to the market and had been listed for only two days when I found it.

I toured the property from top to bottom and made an offer (contingent on an inspection and financing) that same day. Four weeks later, I owned the triplex, and just five weeks after closing, I had successfully rented all the units, and it was generating a significant positive monthly cash flow.

Admittedly, I probably made a mistake during the acquisition process. I was so eager to buy a new-construction property that I didn't make a low offer. Instead, I made an offer really close to the asking price, and it was immediately accepted. Undoubtedly, I left money on the table and could likely have acquired this building for less. Moreover, I knew that the seller was motivated because another purchase was pending and an earlier deal had not materialized. If indicators like these exist, you should offer well below the asking price to see if your bid will be accepted. Well, it's all water under the bridge today. The numbers were very good even at the asking price, and I wasn't sure whether or not there were other prospective buyers waiting in the wings. You often need to trust your instincts in these matters and know value when you see it. If you believe a building is well priced based on your stringent analysis, you should make an aggressive offer (even if it's at or near the asking price) if you can financially justify that price.

My general rule of thumb is that a property should generate a positive monthly cash flow within 90 days from the closing, and, indeed, this one did.

Lessons Learned

- As a buyer, you must learn as much as possible about the seller's motivation for disposing of their property. You must determine why he is selling, if he requires a quick sale, if he is flexible on pricing, and if he is truly motivated and needs to sell. You should target motivated sellers willing to accept a discount in price. This discount from true market value represents your immediate equity in the property and helps to bolster your cash flow.
- You must also do your homework for each potential new acquisition. You can obtain most of this information from the following sources:
  1. The listing agent
  2. The owner
  3. The tenants
  4. Neighbors
  5. The postal delivery agent
  6. The assessor's office
  7. ISD (Inspectional Service's Department)
  8. The local building department
  9. The police department
  10. Local property management companies

- Information is the most valuable asset for any investor.
- After determining whether the seller is motivated, you can modify the offer accordingly. The more motivated the seller, the less you should offer.
- You should try to target motivated sellers because they will accept a price less than market. The equity you have in the property is the difference between the true market value and the price you pay for it; therefore, the less you pay, the more equity you have.
- Once your offer is accepted, you'll have sufficient time to conduct a thorough due diligence on the property. You should also include a financing contingency in the sales contract that will allow you to exit from the deal should you not be able to obtain bank financing for the acquisition. If the property fails the inspection or you are unable to obtain financing, the escrow agent must refund your entire deposit.

Date: November 2002

Total rental units: 6
Value of rental properties: $840,000

5

Third Income-Producing Property

The man who knows "how" will always have a job.
The man who knows "why" will always be his boss.
—RALPH WALDO EMERSON

February 2003

Although it had been only eight months since I had acquired my first apartment building, a licensed appraiser determined that property had appreciated substantially in value. Thanks to the red-hot Boston real estate market, I was able to extract some of the equity from my first income-producing property to buy my third rental property. This time, however, I learned that one could avoid PMI (private mortgage insurance; the insurance payments required of individuals who deposit less than 20 percent of the purchase price at closing) by applying for two loans—one for 80 percent of the purchase price and another one (a piggyback loan) for 10 percent. I would then need to invest only 10 percent of the asking price while still avoiding paying the requisite penalties (i.e., PMI). This would also allow me to keep more funds in my bank account and buy more properties in the future.

By extracting $42,000 from my first building with an equity loan, I was in a position to acquire building #3! At this time, I had been speaking with another landlord friend of mine who was also a member of the Landlord and Investor Group, a club that I founded in 2002. He had had a terrible experience managing the tenants in one of his buildings. After just 16 months of ownership, he wanted out of the landlord business, and he wanted out fast. After he shared with me the horrific stories of the past few months, I asked him if he'd consider selling his property to me. We negotiated a below-market price, given that he'd avoid the broker's 5 percent commission and wanted to sell immediately. I was thus able to acquire a property directly from a motivated seller at a tremendous discount.

These are the types of deals you need to find as a buyer. Savvy investors make their money at the closing table. They buy undervalued properties from motivated sellers, thus creating instant equity from day one. They also network with as many people as possible to find the best possible deals. Let people know that you are in the business of buying real estate, and you'll be amazed by the amount of deal flow that comes your way.

After closing on property #3, I made some minor improvements to the building and was able to resolve the tenant situation. Buying mismanaged properties is another way to make money. Investors who learn how to manage investment properties properly, find good tenants, manage risk, improve the property's appearance, reduce expenses, and increase revenue will be rewarded handsomely in the end. If you know how to detect undervalued assets and have great resolve in managing the turnaround of a rental building, a challenging property for some investors is an absolute financial windfall for others.

Lessons Learned

- As a general rule of thumb, always try to buy properties with as little of your own money as possible without being overleveraged (i.e., resulting in a negative cash flow situation).

Third Income-Producing Property

- If the property still generates a decent positive cash flow with 10 percent down, then you should put only 10 percent down at the time of the purchase. If you can acquire the property for less and still make the numbers work (I essentially bought my buildings with nothing down because I used the equity in my existing properties to buy more rental units. After servicing all three loans, the property still generated a positive cash flow), then by all means buy the property that way.
- Don't assume too much debt on a property if it can't carry itself with the rental income it generates. If you take equity from one property to buy another, you must factor in the increased costs of servicing a larger mortgage or a new equity and piggyback loan.

Date: February 2003

Total rental units: 9

Value of rental properties: $1,258,000

6

Fourth Income-Producing Property

Write it on your heart that every day is the best day in the year.

—RALPH WALDO EMERSON

Believe it or not, there was still equity remaining in investment property 1. Withdrawing more funds from that property would allow me to make a 10 percent down payment on a fourth building, so I began searching again.

My real estate mentor had repeatedly suggested that I buy properties in the same area. The first three properties were no more than a mile away from one another. In fact, I could visit all three of them in less than 10 minutes. The geographical proximity, or clustering, of my rentals made it much easier to manage my growing portfolio.

One morning during the spring of 2003, I received a call from a lawyer who happened to know that I was searching for residential multi-family properties in a particular neighborhood. He had been assigned a property (a three-unit apartment building) that was in receivership. The government sometimes obtains properties that have been abandoned by their owners. These properties might pose a significant danger to the general public because they've been abandoned and lack regular maintenance and general upkeep. The city takes control of these properties, renovates them, brings them up to code, and sells them (typically for below-market rates). The government isn't necessarily in the real estate business, however; it is in the business of assuring that there is a supply of decent housing and that this housing generates income in the form of real estate taxes. The difference between the final sales price of the building and the renovation costs is given to the original owner. As you can imagine, there's no real incentive to maximize the owner's return, since he abandoned the property in the first place; thus, these types of opportunities can be very profitable for an investor.

The lawyer who made me aware of this opportunity put me in contact with the appropriate authorities to obtain more details regarding the sale. Within five minutes of the property tour, I realized that the small apartment building met all of my acquisition criteria. It had off-street parking; a small yard; new plumbing, roof, and heating systems; and a solid foundation, and it was located in a nice neighborhood near public transportation on a street where the majority of the properties were owner-occupied. Most important, I was dealing with a motivated seller willing to accept a below-market rate for the property. As with the other properties, I immediately submitted an offer, negotiated the final price, and closed a month later.

One issue that concerned me a great deal was the building's de-lead certification status. Although the property had been completely renovated, the authorities selling the building would not provide a letter of compliance. I was, however, granted the right to inspect the property (at my own expense) for traces of lead. Upon receiving the letter of compliance from a licensed inspector, I moved forward with the purchase of the property.

De-leading is critical in most states because children under six years of age who eat paint chips containing lead can be seriously harmed. Lead was used in interior and exterior paint before 1978 and is dangerous when ingested. All properties that have not been de-leaded pose a potential health hazard to very young children. It can be extremely expensive to de-lead an apartment, so if you're considering an older property, I suggest that you have the seller provide you with a letter of compliance. Alternatively, you should include in your budget the cost of de-leading the units.

A letter of compliance is a legal document indicating that there are no lead paint hazards and that the property (usually identified by the specific unit) has been successfully de-leaded. A licensed lead inspector issues these documents and assumes responsibility for their accuracy. A letter of interim control (not to be confused with the letter of compliance) indicates only that the work required to make the property temporarily safe from lead hazards has been completed. It is good for only 12 months but can be renewed for a second year. You have to fully de-lead the property and obtain a letter of compliance before the end of the second year. It's best to obtain a letter of compliance before the closing. A property can fall out of compliance if there is chipping paint anywhere on the premises, so you must be sure to address those issues as they appear.

Lessons Learned

- Use the equity in your existing properties to expand your holdings. Small-property owners as well as billionaire real estate landlords do it this way as well.
- If you can leverage your existing properties and still increase your overall cash flow (taking into account the increased expense of servicing the additional equity lines), you should continue to use this strategy over and over again.
- Don't rule out any source of information that can lead you to valuable investment opportunities. Lawyers, government agencies, brokers, other real estate investors, and so on can introduce you to the information you need to generate wealth. Make everyone you know aware of your interest in buying good rental properties.
- It's up to you to act on the information given to you and to turn new acquisitions into profit centers.
- Always determine if a property has been de-leaded, weigh your risks accordingly, and request the appropriate documents before closing.

- If you're buying a property with three bedrooms or more, you should anticipate housing young children. Don't discriminate against families with children who are less than six years of age.

Date: June 2003

The condo was sold in 2003, thereby eliminating all equity lines used in the acquisition of properties 1 and 2.
Total rental units: 12
Value of rental properties: $1,800,000

By this time, I was finally making more in rental income than I was at my day job. After spending countless months analyzing my cash flow and successfully stabilizing my expenses, I was prepared for the transition. It was with great hesitation that I left the "security" of my day job and its weekly paycheck. However, the economics had finally justified my departure, and I could leave on my own terms. In other words, I could survive (barring any unforeseen financial disaster) and pay all of my mortgages and expenses with the income generated by my properties. I wanted to focus my full, undivided attention on building my real estate portfolio, so I bid a bittersweet farewell to my day job and dedicated 100 percent of my time to real estate. I had purchased my first investment property in June 2002. By April 2004, I was generating sufficient after-tax cash flow from my rental properties to leave the 9-to-5 world. I accomplished this feat in less than two years and was thrilled at the prospect of no longer having to work for someone else.

7

Finding the Deals

Lazy hands make a man poor, but diligent hands bring wealth.

—PROVERBS 10:4

Before starting your search for income-producing properties, you should have a very good idea of what you want. If you buy a residential multifamily property (four units or fewer) rather than a commercial multifamily property (five units or more), the requirements for the down payment are substantially less stringent. You will need a minimum down payment of between 20 and 25 percent to acquire a commercial property. When you buy a residential property, banks are far more lenient, so you can buy for as little as 0 to 20 percent down. I would recommend starting your investment career with a residential property of three or four units so that you can learn the business of being a landlord without being too overwhelmed. Residential properties are also much more manageable because of their size and financial requirements. Unfortunately, they won't generate either the level of return or the cash flow that larger commercial apartment buildings tend to produce. Nevertheless, a property of three or four units is an ideal size because you'll be able to finance the acquisition with a relatively small down payment and still have the possibility of generating a positive cash flow.

Let's review some of the criteria you'll need to consider to find the perfect investment property.

Location

When I started investing, I had a 30-minute-drive rule. What does that mean? Well, I tried not to buy properties located more than 30 minutes away from my primary residence. If I had to drive more than half an hour to arrive at one of my buildings, it made the management of the property significantly more difficult. Today, I acquire properties all over the country, but I recommend that you adhere to the 30-minute rule when you are learning the business. If, for example, there is a tenant emergency that needs to be addressed or rental showings to attend, you don't want to spend more than 30 minutes commuting to and from the property. Also, it helps to cluster all your properties in the same vicinity. You run the risk of having all of your eggs in one basket, but the efficiencies you gain (i.e., it's easier to manage and visit all the properties at once) far outweigh the potential disadvantages.

Safety

I also don't buy in areas that I don't feel safe or comfortable visiting. If it's a good deal on paper, but I feel threatened or concerned by the property's location, then it's simply not worth risking my life for the additional cash flow. Unless you have a full-time manager in place, you'll have to visit the property on a regular basis, so be forewarned.

Some investors claim that they would not consider a property if they themselves were not willing to live there. I don't believe this is a prudent or reasonable strategy. If you can't afford or can't find anything worthwhile to buy in a "good" neighborhood, then you should search in areas that are acceptable to you, but more affordable and perhaps less exclusive than you're accustomed to. In fact, there's typically much more money to be made in the less gentrified parts of town than in the more prestigious locations. The price per unit is far less, and the rent you'll obtain in middle-class or poorer parts of town is not proportionally different. You might be able to rent a three-bedroom unit in a poorer neighborhood for $1,500 a month, and an apartment of equivalent size in a well-to-do area might rent for $2,200. However, the purchase price is so substantially different that you'll generate a positive cash flow in the former location and have to pay out of pocket to carry the property in the latter. Still, buying properties in a dangerous part of town just because the numbers work well might not be a wise decision. You need to balance the pros with the cons and make decisions that work best for you.

Competition

It's important to prevent your emotions from playing a decisive role in your decision-making process. Don't focus only on rental properties that meet your personal criteria. Remember that you are not the tenant; you're just the person who collects the rent. Tenants in low-rent areas don't need Kohler toilets, fixtures from Water Works, and granite countertops. Be sure to know what the market expects so that your units are competitive with other housing options on the market. Your rents should also be in line with the current market rates for the area. Read the local Sunday paper to gauge rents, look online (Craigslist.org) to see what others are asking in rent for similar properties, and ask other landlords (join local landlord groups to meet them) what they are charging. Keep up to date on your market, and don't get taken by surprise if no one wants to lease your apartment because you're asking $200 more than everyone else.

Exit Strategy

Rental property owners need to position their properties so that they have the best possible chance for a quick and profitable sale if necessary. Sometimes a dynamic in the market will justify the sale of a rental property. Maybe condo developers are targeting the neighborhood or school districts are changing or highways are being constructed nearby. You might simply want to sell your apartment building and make an upgrade to a larger building with better returns. Be prepared with multiple exit strategies because you never know when you might want to liquidate.

Undervalued Properties

Most communities, even some of the more affluent ones, have some distressed properties or fixer-uppers. A distressed property is one that has been poorly maintained and consequently has a lower market value than other properties in the immediate area. To properly evaluate whether the property is a good investment, you'll need to find the sales prices of comparable properties as well as crunch the numbers to determine the capitalization rate, cash flow, cash-on-cash return, and so on (see Chapter 8, "Evaluating the Deals"). Because renovation expenses will affect your return, you'll need to include these costs in your evaluation.

It is a good idea to find a cosmetic fixer-upper that can be completely renovated with a bit of paint, new floors, new appliances, and a bit of landscaping. Unless you are in the construction business, you should avoid run-down apartment buildings that require major structural repairs. Properties that are priced extremely low probably need everything, and you won't be able to manage this type of project if you're new to the business. The best strategy for a new investor who is looking for a good deal is to find the least desirable property (but one that requires cosmetic repairs only) located in the most desirable neighborhood and owned by a motivated seller.

Investment properties are typically priced less than their true potential market value if they fall into one or all of the following categories:

- The property is owned by a frustrated landlord.
- Rents are too low (beneath market rates).
- The property has a high vacancy rate.
- The building is poorly managed.
- The building requires significant repairs.

In the next chapter, I discuss how to evaluate deals. You'll learn that the revenue that an income-producing property generates less its operating expenses helps to determine its market value. So, it makes sense that if the rents are too low or the expenses are too high, the valuation will be less than optimal. In other words, you can increase the market value of any investment property by managing it better than the previous landlord did. With minor renovations, better landlord/tenant relations, and improved operations, you can increase the rents while reducing the operating expenses and, thus, increase the value of the property. You'll need to conduct a thorough evaluation of a property to determine if any of these factors exist. If you decide that a property can be managed better, it might be an ideal investment should you have what it takes to help the property reach its full economic potential.

Buying Value

To be successful, you must not only buy properties that produce positive cash flow, but also purchase them with positive equity. What do I mean by this? Well, when buying a property, you should try to buy it for less than the actual market value. That way, you instantly make money at the closing table. To accomplish this goal, you must seek out, find, and negotiate the purchase of properties from motivated sellers. Finding motivated sellers and negotiating profitable deals is a full-time job. But the difference between really successful investors and the rest of the pack is their ability to find opportunities that others can't locate. Those who say, "I can't find anything worth buying because the market is too competitive" simply aren't looking hard enough. If you don't make an effort to locate these deals, other investors (who are hungrier than you) will find them. Great deals rarely, if ever, just fall into your lap. There's an abundance of really profitable deals out there, but you have to actually work to find them.

Why, then, are some individuals motivated to sell their properties for less than the true market value?

- The need for the proceeds to acquire another property
- Divorce
- Death or retirement
- Bankruptcy
- Burnout (frustrated landlord)

All of these situations and many more can cause a person to sell his property for less than it's actually worth. All of these circumstances are life-changing (or life-ending) and may pose serious problems for an owner of an income-producing property. Try not to buy a property from an individual who is not at all motivated to sell. Remember, you're searching for deals that provide you with positive equity and cash flow—not more headaches and problems that don't generate profits.

Many investors spend their time looking for the next acquisition. When they find the perfect property, then they determine how much money is needed for the down payment. If they don't have the liquid funds on hand, they must obtain an equity line from one or more of their existing properties, or they must sell one or more of their buildings in order to make the next acquisition. They might be working on a tight deadline and need the proceeds from the sale in order to close (perhaps on a more profitable venture). This situation might cause the seller to become motivated to sell quickly and can be an opportunity for you to buy at a discount.

Many landlords simply leave their income-producing properties to their heirs (spouses and children) upon their demise. Most often, their families have no idea how to manage the rental properties and prefer to simply sell them rather than manage them as a business. Networking with lawyers (especially those who deal with probate law) and financial advisors who specialize in estate planning can be another good source of deals.

Those who file for bankruptcy and allow their properties to deteriorate are another source of stellar opportunities. By joining your local landlord and investor clubs, you'll be able to network with other investors. In time, you should be able to determine if any of them are ready to throw in the towel. If so, you should ask them to consider selling their properties to you. If an investor is able to sell his properties directly to another investor, he'll avoid paying broker commissions. These fees can amount to almost 6 percent of the purchase price, which equates to tens of thousands of dollars. These savings should help you to negotiate a more favorable purchase price! Furthermore, investors are willing to sell at a discount if they believe that you are a serious investor with the capital and ability to close. If you have the financing in place and can conduct your due diligence in a way that won't disrupt the current tenants or property, then the owner may be willing to accept a reduced price. A quick and easy sale is worth a significant discount in price to some property owners. Also, if a relatively new investor has had a terrible experience with his tenants and simply wants a quick exit, he might be willing to negotiate on price if he can expeditiously end his responsibilities as a landlord. As mentioned, I was able to purchase my third property in precisely this manner.

You can typically find frustrated landlords at your local county court-house. The courts schedule housing-related issues on a regular basis. Most of these cases are eviction-related. You are allowed to attend these hearings and watch the proceedings. You may even approach these land-lords as they leave the courtroom and give them your business card. There are distinct and obvious advantages to introducing yourself to a frustrated landlord while he is attempting to evict a tenant. The obvious advantage is that you're catching him at a vulnerable point in time, when he might be at his wits' end and ready to sell a troubled property. You are going to be his savior, but you'll buy only if you can negotiate a favorable price.

How to Get Motivated Sellers to Come to You

Either you can spend your time trying to find motivated sellers, or you can make them find you. With an effective marketing program, you can reach out to these individuals, and they will contact you. The ultimate goal is to have a continuous flow of property owners calling you with new investment opportunities. The more choices you have, the better off you'll be. A thorough marketing plan should include the following.

Postcard Campaigns

Send preprinted postcards to owners of buildings in your target area. Be sure to include the following information:

- "Are you interested in selling your property?"
- "I buy rental properties."
- Your name
- Company name
- Phone number
- Fax number

- E-mail address
- Web site
- "Please contact me at your earliest convenience!"

Knocking on the Doors of Properties You Like

Visit your target area and knock on the doors of the properties that meet your requirements. If it's a non-owner-occupied building, ask the tenants who the owner is and how to contact him. More often than not, the owner or property manager has a sign with his name and contact information posted either on the front of the building or just inside the front door. By law, this contact information must be posted in a visible location in case there should be an emergency. Furthermore, many owners place "for rent" signs on the front of their buildings. The smart ones leave a sign on the building regardless of whether they have vacancies because they will be able to continuously gauge the demand for rentals and obtain prospective tenants for that building or others they might own through the phone calls that the sign generates. Either way, you'll be able to call the phone number listed and inquire about the owner's interest in selling his property.

Mailing Lists

Many companies sell mailing lists of apartment building owners (search in Google for mailing lists + apartment buildings + your desired town). In fact, some organizations have mailing lists for all owners of multifamily property, separated by town and by property size (two-family, three-family, four-family, and so on). For a reasonable price, these organizations will e-mail or mail you a list of what you need. You can "farm" an entire town and send all owners a simple one-page letter of introduction about yourself while inquiring about their property.

Online

Most landlord groups have electronic newsletters and Web sites. For a small fee, you can place an ad on these sites or sponsor these newsletters. The benefit of targeting these groups is that their audience is very specific. You'll be reaching other landlords and investors who already own income-producing properties. Or, they might know someone who might con-

sider selling his properties. Go to http://www.creonline.com/clubs.htm
to find a list of real estate investment clubs in your area.

Newspaper Ads

Placing an ad in a local newspaper can generate a good number of leads.
Be sure to state your interest in buying apartment buildings and insert
your contact information. If possible, place your ad in the "apartments
for rent" or "income properties for sale" section.

> *I buy income-producing properties.*
> *Searching for a 3 or 4 unit apartment building in Miami.*
> *Call Matt Martinez at 555.555.5555 or*
> *email me at matt@landlordandinvestor.com.*

Tracking the effectiveness of each campaign and medium used is
important. Repeat the initiatives that are working and stop the ones that
fail to generate any leads.

The Numbers Game

If you aren't up for the challenge of searching for highly motivated sellers,
you can always play the numbers game and make numerous offers on different properties until a motivated seller agrees to your less-than-mar-
ket-rate offer. For example, if a property has been on the market for more
than 100 days, the owners could be desperate. Ask your broker to print
you a list of all the properties that meet your specific criteria and that
have been listed for 100 days or more. Then take a tour of the properties
and make a very low offer. You'd be surprised just how motivated a seller
might be if his property has been listed for more than three months!
Timing is everything, and if you're able to find an owner who doesn't
want to spend another month paying the mortgage, taxes, and property
expenses, you might be able to obtain a wonderful deal at a substantial
discount. Some investors, including myself, admit that finding moneymaking properties boils down to making several offers. Perhaps you'll
tour 100 properties, and you'll make offers on 50 of them, and maybe,

just maybe, you'll close on one. Although it may take a while for you to find one good deal, it will undoubtedly be a very wise investment that will generate a significant positive cash flow.

Sources for investment properties are:

- Real estate brokers and sales agents
- Wholesalers
- Online Web sites
- Other landlords and property owners
- Newspapers
- People who interact with property owners: lawyers, bankers, government officials, postal agents, inspectors, contractors, electricians, plumbers, constables, and police officers

Real Estate Brokers and Sales Agents

I've purchased properties through brokers, friends, and lawyers and by directly soliciting owners of rental properties. I don't pride myself on buying for top dollar. In fact, I pride myself on paying as little as possible.

Brokers have a good amount of deal flow. They obtain the listings, and they are made aware of properties when they come on the market. After all, this is what they do for a living. The only problems are that everyone else also uses these resources to find deals, and some brokers list their properties for top dollar (especially in hot markets). You are sometimes better off looking elsewhere.

When brokers obtain a listing, they typically schedule an open house for other real estate brokers on a Thursday and hold an open house for the public on Sunday. Oftentimes, an entire week can pass between the time a sales agent receives a listing and the time it is placed on the MLS (Multiple Listing Service—the primary database used to list new properties for sale). Savvy investors use this period of time as an opportunity to acquire properties without having to compete with the general market. Real estate brokers often call their best clients when they receive a listing that meets those clients' requirements.

A property listing that is shown to prospective investors but is not yet available on the MLS or to the general public is referred to as a *pocket listing* because it never leaves the "pocket" of the broker/sales agent. Why would a broker do this? Because she can receive the entire sales commission if she both lists the property and introduces the buyer to the situation. A typical sales commission is 5 percent. That means that 2.5 percent of the sales price is given to the listing agent, and 2.5 percent goes to the broker who finds the buyer. If the listing broker is able to find the buyer and make the sale, she doubles her commission (from 2.5 percent to 5 percent). That's enough incentive to make a few calls before listing a property on the MLS, right?

Pocket listings are not technically legal, but they are common practice. If you are able to convince brokers that you're a serious investor and are actively searching for a property, they will place you on their investor list, and, hopefully, you'll hear about the good deals before everyone else. Once you realize that the best properties on the MLS have been reviewed and rejected by several investors, you'll understand the urgency of knowing how the system works. You can find the deal of the century in most cities, but you need to know how and where to look. Successful investors tend to find their properties where nobody else is looking.

Wholesalers

A wholesaler, or "bird dog," is someone who locates properties, places them under contract, and attempts to transfer the right to buy those properties to another investor. Wholesalers are individuals who make a business of finding motivated sellers and of negotiating a transferable Purchase and Sale (P&S) contract with them. Then, before the required closing date, they find a buyer and transfer the right to buy the property to that investor. After negotiating a below-market price for a property, they pass on the right to buy the property or assign the P&S to someone else. The wholesaler requires a payment (a finder's fee) for his services; however, he does all of the hard work for you. If you want to find wholesalers, simply search for them in Google or another search engine. Or, search your local newspaper for ads that often read something like the following:

"We buy all types of properties."

"We want your ugly home."

"Sell us your property."

"We buy homes or buildings. Call John at . . ."

Introduce yourself as an active investor and let the wholesaler know what type of property you'd consider. Wholesalers can save you an inordinate amount of time searching for and negotiating deals. They do all the heavy lifting, and they sell at a lower price than you might pay if you found the property through more traditional channels.

Online

As mentioned, the MLS is the private network for licensed real estate agents. If you are not a licensed agent, then you do not have access to the MLS network (unless, of course, you ask your friendly real estate agent for his password and user ID). Realtor.com is the official Web site of the National Association of Realtors, so all of the properties listed on the MLS are also listed online at www.realtor.com. Realtor.com is available to the general public, and anyone with Internet access may consult the database. For the reasons already mentioned, I don't spend too much time buying properties that are listed on the MLS or Realtor.com. I would rather search for new deals where the majority of investors aren't looking.

LoopNet (www.loopnet.com) is the largest Web site listing all commercial real estate property categories, including commercial office space, industrial, multifamily (apartments), and retail. The site is open to the general public, but some listings are hidden if you don't pay the monthly membership fee of about $50. Most properties are commercial (five units or more), but you can also find some smaller multifamily apartment buildings (four units or fewer).

Craigslist (www.craigslist.org) is an extremely popular Web site with locally targeted sites for each city. The "properties for sale" section is updated daily by investors and brokers who want to sell properties. You should conduct a search for "investment properties" to find prospective candidates.

In fact, Craigslist allows you to upload your own ad. You might consider placing an ad in the "properties for sale" or the "rentals" section expressing your interest in buying rental properties. Indicate what you are looking for and the price range and neighborhood. Your principal objective is to fill and constantly maintain your pipeline of opportunities.

Other Landlords and Property Owners

One of the very best ways to buy properties at a discount is to buy them from other landlords. Expand your network by joining investment clubs and introducing yourself to other investors in your area. Perhaps you'll find a property owner who is tired of being a landlord, wants to retire from the business, or simply plans to sell his rentals to upgrade to larger properties. If you can eliminate the broker's commission, you'll be in a very good position to reduce the selling price because the owner won't have to pay these fees. Moreover, if you can eliminate the pain of selling a property by offering a quick sale and a short, noninvasive due diligence period, the owner might be further inclined to sell at a discount. Aggressively pursue other landlords and make them aware of your intention and ability to buy their properties should they be inclined to sell.

Newspapers

For nearly every property for sale, whether it's a broker MLS listing, a LoopNet listing, or a FSBO (for sale by owner), the seller or his representatives typically market the property in local newspapers. You should review the Sunday paper on a regular basis and highlight the properties that appeal to you. You might even call a few of the individuals listed in the ads to introduce yourself and let them know who you are and the type of property that you are interested in acquiring. They might have more properties that they would consider selling but that they hadn't placed on the market yet. Also, call ads that list properties for rent but don't list a real estate brokerage firm. Brokerage firms are required to indicate the name of their company along with the properties they are representing in all newspaper ads. If the name doesn't appear, you'll be calling either the owner himself or the property manager. Introduce yourself and, once again, inquire as to his interest in selling properties that meet your requirements.

People Who Interact with Property Owners

Who else is informed when properties are about to be put up for sale? Ask yourself the following question: when I want to sell my home, whom do I inform first? You probably tell your lawyer, your accountant, your friends, your electrician or plumber (if you need to make repairs before the sale), and perhaps your banker. Investors who own income-producing properties are no different. A number of individuals are made aware of sales opportunities because of their direct relationship with property owners. Also, they are privy to information because of their field of work. If an investor has defaulted on his loan, lawyers and bankers are the first to learn about this unique opportunity. If you know the lawyers and bankers, you might be second in line to receive valuable information about a pending sale. Constables deal with evictions, and they might know a landlord who is tired of dealing with bad tenants and is ready to sell. Plumbers do a lot of work for several landlords each and every week. They know who is struggling and who might consider selling. Don't discount any of your contacts—and be sure they know what type of property you want.

Making the Offer

When making an offer, submit a price that is well below the asking price (if, of course, the property isn't already underpriced). This might mean a 10 to 30 percent reduction, depending on how aggressive you want to be. You don't want to offend the seller, but you must negotiate a good deal. Be patient and wait until the seller responds. Perhaps the seller is insulted and won't respond at all. You may risk losing the deal, but he might return in a few weeks if no other offers are submitted. Ask the owner (assuming that you're not working with a broker) what is the least he's willing to accept, and then be extremely silent. Don't say a word. Silence is the most effective negotiating strategy: "He who speaks first always loses." Then, ask if he'd be willing to accept a lower price if you were to close in 30 days (30 days is a sufficient amount of time to obtain financing and run a thorough title search), or if you were to offer specific terms that the owner wants. To be successful with this negotiating strategy, you must know why the owner is selling and what his specific needs are for a successful sale. If you meet his requirements and are flexible with his terms, you'll always be able to negotiate a better price.

When your system to unearth motivated sellers and profitable deals is in place, you'll be in a position to screen all of your opportunities thoroughly and pursue only the biggest moneymakers. Until that time, you'll need to continue to develop the program that works for you and implement some or all of the strategies highlighted in this chapter.

Lessons Learned

- Buy only properties that meet your specific criteria.
- Pursue only deals that make good financial sense and provide a positive cash flow.
- Buy properties only at a discount from their true market value. Deals like these typically come from motivated sellers or from property owners who haven't managed their apartments properly. Otherwise you'll pay market rate, and it's much more difficult to make money buying retail.
- The ideal rental property is different in every town. For example, a triple-decker (a three-family building) in the city is likely to generate significantly more revenue than a similarly priced single-family home in the suburbs.
- Multifamily buildings in low-income areas that are on the rise typically offer significantly better returns than similarly sized buildings in much nicer parts of town. Why is this? Well, the purchase price is often significantly lower, yet the rents might be only marginally different. Moreover, the appreciation realized in up-and-coming neighborhoods tends to surpass that in more gentrified areas.
- Investors should seek a balance between buying in marginal areas with great potential and buying in more established neighborhoods. Try to buy the best deal in the best neighborhood that you can afford. Buying in areas that you understand and are intimately familiar with has its advantages.

8

Evaluating the Deals

I try to learn from the past, but I plan for the future
by focusing exclusively on the present.

—Donald Trump

earning to distinguish a great opportunity from a terrible one can be
challenging if you are unfamiliar with the methods used to determine
value. An untrained eye might see a stellar property without blemishes.
A highly trained eye might see a bevy of problems and a host of reasons
not to buy. As an investor, you must know what to look for and how to
decipher the numbers to make well-informed decisions. Determining
the value of a property is sometimes more of an art than a science, and
appraisers are constantly tweaking the numbers to justify their evalua-
tions. As an investor, you should know all of the methods the industry
uses to determine property value. There are three standard valuation
approaches used in real estate.

Comparable Sales Approach

The price of similar properties sold during the past 6 to 12 months indicates a property's current worth. The sales prices of the comparable properties are adjusted for differences in lot size, livable area, features, garages, number of bedrooms and baths, condition of the property, and location. The goal is to find similar properties that were recently sold so that a realistic price can be assigned to the property in question. Licensed appraisers will evaluate a number of properties and take an average of the adjusted sales prices to determine a fair market value.

Replacement Cost Approach

The replacement cost approach calculates the current cost to rebuild an equivalent structure. The goal with this approach is to determine what it would cost to rebuild the exact same structure on a similar plot of land.

Income Approach (or Capitalization Approach)

The primary method for evaluating income-producing property is the income approach. This approach considers the revenue (rental income) generated by the property and its operating expenses to determine value. The income approach is incredibly useful when determining the value of a property. In fact, it's the primary calculation I use in my analysis of multi-family properties. For single-family homes and condos, I typically use the comparable sales approach, but I use the income approach for apartment buildings. The income approach uses the capitalization rate (cap rate) to determine property value. The cap rate is the yield or interest rate you would receive if you purchased the property for cash (without a mortgage). Cap rates on investment properties tend to fall between the 10-year Treasury bond yield and current stock market returns. Because the bond yield is currently hovering around 3 percent and stock market returns are less than 8 percent, apartment building yields (or cap rates) of 6 to 7 percent aren't unreasonable at this point in time.

> **Cap rate** = net operating income (NOI)/value of the property (price)
> This formula allows you to determine the cap rate, or the rate of return based on one year's projected net operating income.

Evaluating the Deals

Depending on the property's type, quality, size, age, and location and the inherent risks involved, properties have traded at cap rates between 7 percent and 12 percent. The historical average is somewhere around 9 percent. Fortunately, I was able to purchase my first four investment properties at cap rates well above 10 percent.

Value of the property (price) = NOI/cap rate

Net operating income = total gross operating income − total operating expenses

Total gross operating income = total gross income − vacancy and credit loss

Total gross income is the total gross scheduled rental income if all units were rented and all the rents were collected plus any other income generated by the property (i.e., laundry income, rental parking, garages, vending machines, and so on).

Vacancy is the revenue you lose when your apartments are not occupied by paying tenants. If your potential annual rental income is $50,000 and you have a 5 percent vacancy rate, then you expect to earn only $47,500 for the year because your vacancy loss is $2,500.

Total operating expenses are expenses that are necessary if a property is to continue producing revenue. These expenses include utilities, repairs, management fees, taxes, landscaping, snow removal, and so on. Mortgage payments, capital expenditures, and depreciation are not operating expenses. Operating expenses include any expenses required to maintain and manage the property for one full year.

The operating expenses typically add up to about 30 to 50 percent of the gross operating income. If they are more than 50 percent, your keen management skills can probably lower them to the 30 percent level. If the owner claims that the operating expenses are much less than 30 percent, you should certainly be skeptical.

You should know the average trading cap rate for small apartment buildings in your area, and then you should calculate the building's NOI (net operating income) to determine the market price for the building.

Using the following spreadsheet, you can easily determine a property's NOI.

CASH FLOW TEMPLATE

INCOME

    Gross scheduled (rental) income
    Plus Other income (laundry, parking, etc.)

    Total Gross Income
    Less vacancy and credit loss

    (Annual) Gross Operating Income

OPERATING EXPENSES

    Taxes
    Insurance
    Electricity and gas
    Water and sewer
    Trash removal
    Landscaping and snow removal
    Advertising
    Repairs and maintenance
    Supplies
    Other

    Total Annual Operating Expenses

    Net Operating Income (NOI)

Let's use the following example for illustration purposes:

- A triplex (a three-unit building).
- Generating $4,500 per month or $54,000 per year in rental income.

Evaluating the Deals

- Laundry income equals $100 per month, or $1,200 per year.
- Taxes are $4,000 per year.
- Insurance is $2,000 per year.
- Electricity and gas cost $1,000 per year.
- Water and sewer cost $1,200 per year.
- Trash removal is $400 per year.
- Landscaping and snow removal cost $1,000 per year.
- Advertising equals $300 per year.

TRIPLEX APARTMENT BUILDING NOI ANALYSIS	
INCOME	
Gross scheduled (rental) income	$54,000
Other income (laundry, parking, etc.)	$1,200
Total Gross Income	$55,200
Less vacancy and credit loss (5%)	$2,760
(Annual) Gross Operating Income	$52,440
OPERATING EXPENSES	
Taxes	$4,000
Insurance	$2,000
Electricity and gas	$1,000
Water and sewer	$1,200
Trash removal	$400
Landscaping and snow removal	$1,000
Advertising	$300
Repairs and maintenance	$2,500
Supplies	$500
Other	$0
Total Annual Operating Expenses	$12,900
Net Operating Income (NOI)	$39,540

- Repairs and maintenance are $2,500 per year.
- Supplies are $500 per year.

Assuming that your acceptable rate of return is 9 percent, the value of the property is calculated as follows:

$$NOI/cap\ rate = value\ of\ the\ property$$

Or,

$$\$39,540/0.09 = \$439,333$$

If a 9 percent cap rate were acceptable to you, then you'd be willing to pay $439,333 for the property. Changing the cap rate either up or down will determine your own valuation of the property.

How Different Cap Rates Affect the Value of the Property

11% cap rate = $359,454

10% cap rate = $395,400

8% cap rate = $494,250

7% cap rate = $564,857

6% cap rate = $659,000

The lower the cap rate, the more expensive the property will be to acquire. In a red-hot market with an abundance of demand for apartment buildings, the cap rate will decline as demand increases; therefore, you'll have to pay more for the property, and your returns will diminish accordingly.

As a rule of thumb, I try not to buy anything for less than an 8 percent cap rate. Buying below this rate with 20 percent down at closing usually means that you'll own a property with negative cash flow. If you make a larger down payment, your cash flow will improve, but your cash-on-cash return will decline and your cash reserves will be depleted.

Evaluating the Deals

Because cash is king, I always analyze a property for its cap rate, but I am keenly interested in its cash flow. In other words, does the property make any money at the end of the year? Use the cap rate as a benchmark to compare properties across the board. Use the cash flow analysis to determine if you're actually going to make money each year.

As you will see from the cash flow spreadsheet, it is rather easy to determine a property's cash flow. The most difficult part of this exercise is making sure that the numbers you input into the spreadsheet are accurate. Don't rely on the seller or the broker to provide you with accurate numbers. You should check and double-check the income and expenses that are provided during the due diligence period. Also, you should ask to view all the current leases and make the owner submit certified paperwork that documents all the revenue and expenses. Furthermore, you must call the trash disposal company, landscaper, water and sewer companies, insurance company, taxing authorities, and utility companies to verify the operating expenses. I have known a few dishonest sellers and brokers who inflated the revenue and decreased the expenses to make a building appear more financially attractive. It is your responsibility to make absolutely sure that your analysis is based on reality rather than fiction. In fact, I recommend that you assume that the numbers provided are inaccurate. That way, you won't experience any unpleasant surprises, and you'll be more inclined to verify all the numbers.

The following is a spreadsheet analysis for a three-unit apartment building (a triplex). Assume that the building was purchased at a 9 percent cap rate for $439,333 and that you deposited 10 percent from your savings at closing and received a second (piggyback) loan of 10 percent to purchase the property.

- Purchase price: $439,333
- First loan for 80 percent of purchase price: $351,466 (at a 6 percent interest rate, amortized over 30 years)
- Second loan for 10 percent of purchase price: $43,933 (at an 8 percent interest rate, amortized over 30 years)
- Your down payment of 10 percent of purchase price: $43,933

INCOME	
Gross scheduled rental income	$54,000
Other income (laundry, parking, etc.)	$1,200
Total Gross Income	$55,200
Less vacancy and credit loss (5%)	$2,760
Gross Operating Income	**$52,440**
OPERATING EXPENSES	
Taxes	$4,000
Insurance	$2,000
Utilities (electricity, gas)	$1,000
Water and sewer	$1,200
Trash removal	$400
Landscaping and snow removal	$1,000
Advertising	$300
Repairs and maintenance	$2,500
Supplies	$500
Other	$0
Total annual operating expenses	**$12,900**
Net operating income (NOI)	**$39,540**
DEBT SERVICE	
Annual debt service (first mortgage)	$25,286.64
Annual debt service (second mortgage or home equity line of credit)	$3,868.32
Total annual debt service	**$29,154.96**
CASH FLOW	
Annual cash flow or revenue (before taxes)	$10,385.04

Evaluating the Deals

The four principal financial benchmarks used to evaluate any income-producing property are:

1. *Capitalization rate.*

   Capitalization rate = NOI/value of the property

   Capitalization rate is an investor's rate of return from a property. Use the cap rate formula to compare and contrast income-producing properties of all types.

   $$\$39,540/\$439,333 = 9\%$$
   $$\text{Cap rate} = 9\%$$

2. *Cash-on-cash return.*

   Cash-on-cash return = annual cash flow before taxes/(down payment + any other up-front expenses)

   Cash-on-cash return = $10,385.04/$43,933

   Cash-on-cash return = 23.64 percent (before-tax return)

3. *IRR (the internal rate of return).* Well, the textbook definition for the internal rate of return is the discount rate that makes the net present value of the property's cash flows equal to zero. Are you confused? Don't worry, because it's a number that can easily be determined by using MS Excel or a similar program. No one I know calculates this by hand, though I do remember doing it that way 10 years ago in one of my finance classes in college. The IRR provides a rate of return over a period of time rather than a static rate of return (i.e., cash-on-cash return) at a specific point in time. It takes into consideration both the size and the timing of the property's cash flows as well as the initial investment and the expected future sales price.

4. *DCR (debt coverage ratio) or DSCR (debt service coverage ratio).*

DCR = net operating income/annual debt service

DCR = $39,540/$29,154.96

DCR = 1.356

Banks typically prefer a DCR of 1.2 or higher for most commercial investments.

After evaluating this property by using the rigorous formulas just outlined, I would either

- Accept the building and make an immediate offer.
- Reject this building as a potential new acquisition.
- Reduce the offer price until the numbers meet my guidelines.

What are reasonable guidelines? Well, I tend to use the following three formulas most often to analyze a building of this size:

1. *Cap rate: 8 percent or higher.* This is a reasonable cap rate for rental properties. Don't compete with the condo converters who are buying buildings at 4 percent cap rates (more on this later in the book). Because finding this rate is extremely challenging in some U.S. cities these days, you might want to search in places where the competition is less fierce to obtain the returns you desire. Alternatively, you should employ the advice provided in Chapter 7, "Finding the Deals," to unearth the hard-to-find deals. The property we are evaluating has a 9 percent cap rate.
2. *Cash-on-cash return: 15 percent or higher.* Because I could earn 7.5 percent on my hard-earned money with less risky investments, I hope to at least double that rate (15 percent) in real estate. The cash-on-cash return in this example is nearly 24 percent.
3. *Debt coverage ratio: 1.2 or higher.* At the end of the day, the bank will determine whether or not it wants to lend you the necessary funds to buy the property. Because banks look for a minimum DCR of 1.2, you should use this parameter as well. The DCR for the property under consideration is 1.356.

I was always comfortable if a three-family building provided me with at least one month of rental income in positive cash flow. I figured that even if I had one vacancy in a three-unit building, I would still break even and wouldn't have to feed the property from my own bank account. That was the nonformulaic benchmark that I used in determining whether or not I wanted to acquire a building. If you are considering buying rental properties in a highly sought-after area during times like today, you might have to settle for substantially less. Only you can determine how close you want to come to the break-even level—just as long as you aren't in the red.

At Least Break Even?

Many investors have the goal of breaking even each month. They claim that anything other than a loss is acceptable, and that building equity is more important than generating cash flow each year. This might be acceptable in some markets; however, my strategy has always been to buy properties at the right price so that you make money each and every month. Now, if you live in a high-demand (bubble) area such as Boston, New York City, San Diego, San Francisco, Los Angeles, Washington, D.C., or Miami, a break-even scenario might be acceptable. But, I never buy for anticipated appreciation, and I suggest you don't either. Rather, I buy properties only if they have the potential to provide a positive monthly cash flow in 90 or fewer days. I don't like to subsidize my properties from my own savings. Each building must provide an acceptable monthly cash flow (my salary), and any annual appreciation is simply an ancillary benefit of ownership. It's absolutely critical that you have enough money left over after paying operating expenses and the mortgage to provide you with an income. After all, you are trying to leave your day job by replacing your salary with rental income. If your properties aren't producing a positive cash flow, you'll never be able to leave your job. Stop thinking about appreciation and focus on the cash flow!

What seems like a good deal might, instead, really turn out to be a lemon. An investor needs to be able to analyze properties to determine monthly cash flow, anticipated future cash flows, cash-on-cash return,

IRR, debt coverage ratio, NOI, and the cap rate. All of these formulas allow you to better understand whether you're buying a property for a reasonable price or whether the seller is taking advantage of you.

Don't Forget the Benefits of Depreciation

Depreciation is a noncash expense. It represents a capital reserve for replacing the property (not the land) after it has exhausted its total expected "lifespan." The IRS allows you to depreciate a property over 27.5 years. So, if the basis (not including the value of the land) of your property is $300,000, the annual depreciation will be calculated as follows:

$$\$300,000/27.5 = \$10,909.09 \text{ per year}$$

Therefore, you may deduct $10,909.09 from the earnings of your property before calculating taxes owed.

Lessons Learned

- Don't be a speculator—speculators go broke! Be an investor with a plan!
- Don't buy for appreciation or tax breaks—always buy cash flow. Cash is KING!
- Don't buy properties with negative cash flow when you begin, because you won't survive.
- Know how to evaluate properties for their current market value and return.
- Don't buy properties based on what the seller tells you they are worth. Buy based on actual rental revenue and expenses. If the seller claims that the rents should be $200 a month higher, you should thank him for the information but continue to run your analysis on the actual rents and not pro forma.
- Value for all income-producing properties is based on the capitalization approach.
- As the cap rate goes up, the price of the property goes down. As the cap rate goes down, the price of the property goes up. Fluctuations

in cap rates are beneficial to you only if you are a seller in a compressed cap-rate environment or a buyer in a high-cap-rate environment.

- Buy properties only for the revenue they generate, and run your numbers as accurately as possible to distinguish a good deal from a poor one.
- It is extremely difficult for investors to achieve greater than average gains without assuming greater than average risk. A bad investment is one that exposes you to a higher level of risk than the level of return. To achieve a better return, you must incur more risk.
- If you do your homework thoroughly and execute properly, you will buy properties at the right price, and each of them will generate a positive cash flow that will eventually free you from the responsibilities of your day job.

9

Financing and Acquiring the Deals

A bank is a place that will lend you money if you can prove that you don't need it.

—Bob Hope

All lenders are not created equal, so shop your deal around to as many financial institutions as possible. Loans are available from banks, mortgage companies, mortgage brokers, credit unions, hard-money lenders, and private lenders. Determined to secure the best rate and terms available, I created a spreadsheet analysis of more than 50 lenders to compare my financing options. In this document, I listed each lender's rates, terms, conditions, points required, programs offered, addresses, phone numbers, and contact names. I personally met with nearly all of the lenders to discuss my specific objectives. Some lenders offer lower rates but require you to pay points. Other lenders offer programs without points but demand higher interest rates. Some mortgage brokers offer more options because they work with several lenders but cannot guarantee you the best possible financing. Finding the money at the lowest rate for the program you want with as little up-front costs (points) as possible is preferred. Compare and negotiate all of your loan options, regardless of whether the loan is a first mortgage, a refinancing, or a home equity loan. At the end of the day, however, you should work with a lending institution that will actually deliver the funds you need on time, regardless of whether its rate is the most competitive. After a few years in this business, you learn not to lose too much sleep over ¼ or ½ point of interest. Instead, you learn to stay focused on moving your project forward by obtaining the financing you need.

Rates

The rate for your loan is the annual interest rate you will pay on the money you have borrowed. You'll need to determine whether the rate is fixed or adjustable (variable-rate loans). For fixed-rate loans, 15-, 20-, and 30-year terms are most common. During the life of the loan, the payment due never changes. Generally speaking, the shorter the term of the loan, the lower the interest rate. Adjustable-rate loans typically offer a low starting rate, but that rate will change in the future (rates are typically fixed for one, three, or five years). If interest rates increase after the initial holding period, the amount due each month will also increase. Interest-rate caps do exist to prevent lenders from raising rates excessively. Rates change each day or even several times each day in a volatile market, so be sure to find the most recent rate information. All lenders must provide an APR (annual percentage rate). The APR takes into consideration closing costs, points, broker's fees, and other charges to determine an overall blended rate. The APR allows you to compare all of the programs, regardless of their respective costs and fees.

Points

Points are fees that you pay to secure the loan you desire. They are paid directly to the mortgage broker or lender. Points and rates are inversely related, so when the rate is low, the points tend to increase. When the rates are higher, the points tend to be less. Specifically, 1 point is equal to 1 percent of the total loan amount, and these fees are paid at the closing.

Many programs don't actually require points to be paid, so look for lenders offering this type of program.

Fees

You must pay lenders various fees for providing a mortgage. These fees vary widely and should be analyzed closely. An estimate of all the fees being charged can be found on the good faith estimate (a document that you should request from the lender before closing). The actual fees are listed on your settlement statement at closing. The fees include charges such as the loan origination or underwriting fee; transaction, settlement, attorney, and closing costs; title search and insurance; courier fees; recording fees; and state and local taxes. Don't feel too bad if your attorney receives only $500 for his work. If the attorney selects the title company, he is probably being given a good portion of its fee as a "commission." You should negotiate all of these fees (if possible) with the lender before moving forward because they can add up to thousands of dollars.

Mortgage Programs

Lenders have created several different mortgage options to suit the needs of almost any investor. There are numerous types of financing options available through conventional banks, and the following are the most popular:

1. 30-year fixed-rate mortgage
2. 15-year fixed-rate mortgage
3. 1-, 3-, or 5-year adjustable-rate mortgage (ARM)
4. Interest-only mortgage
5. Option ARM mortgage

I've used nearly all of these types of mortgages to buy property. How do you make a decision about which will work best for you? Well, you should first familiarize yourself with all of your options and then find the best programs being offered.

The 30-year fixed-rate mortgage is the bellwether of the mortgage industry. It is often used as an indicator to compare and contrast historical rates. A 30-year mortgage is amortized over 30 years, meaning that the payments cover both principal and interest until the balance is $0.00. The monthly payments will not change during this time. So, if you hold on to your property for 30 years and never refinance the loan, you'll pay the same amount each month until you own the house outright. This is a very conservative mortgage option. The loan's rate is typically higher than that of alternatives, but the fixed rate provides a great deal of security because your payment will not fluctuate.

The 15-year fixed-rate mortgage is similar to the 30-year fixed-rate mortgage; however, the rate may be slightly lower because the loan is amortized over only 15 years, and so there's less perceived risk for the lender. Your payments will be higher because of the shorter period of amortization; however, you'll be on track to pay back the entire loan in 15 rather than 30 years. As with the 30-year fixed-rate program, the rate and the monthly payments will not change during the life of the loan.

One-, three-, and five-year ARMs are mortgages where the rate is fixed for one to five years and then is adjusted after the end of that period. For instance, a 5/1 ARM offers the mortgagor (the individual who borrows money to purchase real property; the mortgagor provides the lender with a guarantee for the full repayment of the loan) five years of interest and principal payments at a specific rate. After the fifth year, the rate may change every year, depending on market conditions. The initial interest rate is typically less than the rate on a 30- or 15-year fixed-rate mortgage; however, the risk to the individual assuming the loan is higher because the rate after the hold period is unknown. The payments will typically be less up front, but the uncertainty of not knowing what the payments will be after one to five years might offset any initial benefit.

Interest-only programs allow the mortgagor to pay only the interest for a specified period of time (typically 6 months to 10 years); after that period, the borrower must pay principal at an accelerated rate along with the interest portion. The popularity of interest-only mortgages has been growing as property values have skyrocketed during the past few years. Individuals have attempted to decrease their monthly mortgage obligations through this and other mortgage programs. The following chart indicates the percentage of home buyers using these programs and the cities where they are most popular.

San Diego	48%
Atlanta	46%
San Francisco	45%
Denver	43%
Oakland	43%
San Jose	41%
Phoenix	38%
Seattle	37%

SOURCE: LoanPerformance LLC and *BusinessWeek,* June 27, 2005 p. 35

Option ARMs, or option adjustable-rate mortgages, provide borrowers with three payment plans to choose from each month. With option ARMs, the borrower has the flexibility of increasing or decreasing the payment each month. The first option is the most expensive (principal and interest payment). This is similar to a more traditional 30-year fixed or 5-year adjustable program in which the payment covers both interest and principal. Option two is a payment of interest only. Only the interest is paid each month; the principal is not, so the mortgage balance remains the same. Option three is the lowest acceptable payment option and may not even cover the interest, resulting in the overall loan balance increasing, depending on the fluctuation of rates. The difference between the actual payment made and the interest due is added to the mortgage balance (this is referred to as negative amortization). Depending on your expenses and bank reserves, this option provides you with an enormous amount of flexibility to pay what you can afford each month, but it comes with the risk of an ever-increasing mortgage balance.

You should know how much your monthly payment will increase and at what interval the changes can occur if you are working with a loan that is not fixed. Also, you'll need to determine whether the potential increased payments are going to be manageable. Although the rates are initially less with a variable-rate loan, not knowing what your future payments will be might offset the benefits enjoyed during the first few years.

Figures 9.1 and 9.2 provide an example of the various mortgage programs and their corresponding monthly payments, given a purchase

		Pros	Cons
Price of property	$ 500,000.00		
20% down	$ 100,000.00		
Mortgage	$ 400,000.00		
30-year fixed-rate mortgage at 6%	$ 2,398.00	Never have to worry about your mortgage changing. Best for low-risk individuals. Interest rate stays the same over 30-year period of time.	High monthly payment. Greatest amount of interest paid from all mortgage options.
15-year fixed-rate mortgage at 5.5%	$ 3,268.00	Pay off loan sooner. Interest rate stays the same for 15 years. Less interest paid than the 30-year program.	Highest possible payment option per month.
5/1 adjustable-rate mortgage or ARM at 4.5%	$ 2,027.00	Lower payments. Fixed payments/rate for 5 years. 1-, 3-, 7- and 10-year options exist. Best if you are going to liquidate or refinance the property before the 5th year.	Rate and payment can change after the 5th year. Amortized over a 30-year period of time.
Interest-only mortgage for 30-year fixed at 4%	$ 2,000.00	Low payment for the first 10 years with no payment of principal. Low payments for several years.	Higher payments after the 10th year with principal payments added. No mortgage reduction through payments for 10 years.
Interest-only mortgage for a 5/1 ARM at 4.1%	$ 1,375.00	Lowest possible payment option per month. Fixed rate for the first 5 years.	After the 5th year, the rate adjusts each year. Higher payments after the 10th year with principal payments added. No mortgage reduction through payments for 10 years.

Figure 9.1 Different Mortgage Types and Payments

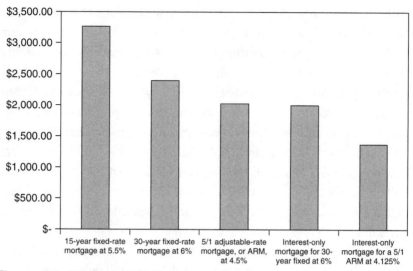

Figure 9.2 Mortgage Options

price of $500,000 and a down payment of 20 percent, with the remaining balance of $400,000 being financed.

Some lenders might offer more competitive interest rates and charge points, but these rates are indicative of current market conditions. I did not include the option ARM in Figures 9.1 and 9.2 because programs of this type vary dramatically, and it's difficult to determine the monthly payment. Some lenders and/or brokers offer starter rates as low as 1 percent for the first 12 months and increase the rate significantly afterward.

I don't recommend using the 15-year fixed-rate mortgage. If you want to pay off your mortgage in 15 years, then simply use a 30-year option and make extra payments toward principal. If you are a disciplined investor, this strategy will work for you. There's no need to lock yourself into higher payments when you can accomplish the same goal with a more flexible 30-year option (just adhere to the accelerated payment plan).

When I first starting buying properties, I opted for the 30-year fixed-rate mortgage because this option gave me the greatest security for the long term. I would have classified myself as a conservative and inexperienced investor who thought that I'd hold onto each of my properties for the next 100 years. I used a 5-year ARM to purchase the last two triplexes because I don't anticipate holding the properties for more than 5 years.

These programs allowed me to lock in a rate for a sufficient period of time while minimizing my carrying costs. Because cash flow is so critical during the early years of ownership, I decided to improve my bottom line while I worked diligently to reduce operating expenses and increase rental revenue. Also, if you intend to sell your properties or refinance them to acquire more properties, then locking in a 30-year fixed-rate mortgage at a higher interest rate will cost you more money during the time you hold the loan. If you plan to hold the property for 1, 3, 5, or 30 years, then you should consider all the programs and select the one that works best for you. Ultimately, you need to decide what your risk tolerance is and select a plan that meets your financial objectives without compromising your ability to sleep at night.

For more information regarding loans and programs, you should consult your mortgage broker or bank as well as the following sites:

Fannie Mae: www.fanniemae.com

Freddie Mac: www.freddiemac.com

Federal Housing Administration: www.hud.gov

www.realtors.org

www.responsiblelending.org

You should also review your credit report to make sure it is accurate. If there are any errors in your report, it can affect your ability to obtain a loan. There are three credit bureaus that will provide you with this information. They are:

TransUnion: (800) 888-4213

Experian: (888) 397-3742

Equifax: (800) 685-1111

According to NREI (May 2005, p. 50, "NREI's Top 40" www.nreonline.com), the country's largest commercial lenders are the following:

1. Bank of America $58.6 billion
2. Wachovia $46.8 billion
3. KeyBank $18.8 billion
4. GMAC $17.1 billion

5. Lehman Brothers $16.5 billion
6. CSFB $12.5 billion
7. LaSalle Bank $11.5 billion
8. Morgan Stanley $11.1 billion
9. Washington Mutual $9.9 billion
10. GE Commercial $8.1 billion

Sources for the Down Payment

Now that you've learned more about mortgage programs, you'll need to consider how to come up with the funds for the down payment. The required down payment could range between 0 and 25 percent of the purchase price (depending on several factors including whether you're a first-time home buyer, whether the property will be owner occupied, and whether it is a residential building with fewer than five units or a multi-family commercial property with five units or more). If the property is 100 percent financed, you need not concern yourself with the following few paragraphs. If it is not, then you'll need to secure the down payment funds before the closing.

The following is a list of the main sources of these funds.

Banks

Some banks offer small-business loans sponsored by the SBA. Some of these loans aren't secured by existing assets, thus making it easier to obtain funding. Some banks and credit unions offer direct business or personal loans that you can use for the down payment. Other lending institutions have small-business programs that offer lines of credit at favorable rates and terms. These loans can be used to grow your business (i.e., to buy more property). Inquire at all of your local banks and lending institutions about their specific programs. The application is typically only a few pages long, and you'll receive a response from the lender within a few weeks. Some banks offer as much as $100,000 with a low-document-verification approval. In other words, you can obtain these funds by completing a simple three-page application. Funds in excess of the low-document limit require more extensive due diligence on the part of the lending institution, so you might have to submit tax forms and banking documents.

All of these lenders want your business; thus, they are willing to lend you $30,000, $50,000, or $100,000 to establish a banking relationship with your company. They might request that you establish a savings or checking account with a minimum deposit, but this is a small price to pay for the funds you need. The monthly loan payments can be directly withdrawn from the savings or checking account you establish with the lender.

Home Equity Loan

Taking a home equity loan on the existing equity in your primary residence or investment property is another source for the down payment. Find a lender that will provide a competitive rate with no up-front fees. Also, be careful, because some institutions will charge a penalty fee (several hundred dollars) if you close the loan in less than the specified time (typically two to three years). The lender will need to make an appraisal of your property and will typically lend up to 80 percent LTV (loan to value). In other words, if you own a property that is worth $500,000 and your mortgage is $300,000, the bank will not just lend you the difference ($200,000). Instead, it calculates 80 percent of the appraised value ($500,000 $\times$ 0.80 = $400,000) and reduces that amount by the outstanding debt ($400,000 − $300,000 = $100,000). The bank will lend you the surplus equity of $100,000. Your mortgage and monthly payments do not change. Furthermore, you can use the $100,000 to buy more property or to pay off credit cards, medical expenses, or other consumer debt. The interest paid on the equity loan is even tax-deductible. If you don't need all the money in one lump sum, then you can obtain a line of credit. The bank will issue you a checkbook that you can use for the entire account. The payment due each month is based on a calculation of the outstanding balance. In other words, you are not charged interest on the full $100,000 if you have a line of credit and you have used only $25,000. You are required to pay interest only on the amount of money outstanding.

Cash-Out Refinancing

You can always refinance your property and withdraw the difference between your current mortgage balance and the new refinanced amount (thus the term *cash-out* refinancing). For example, let's assume (as in the previous example) that your property is worth $500,000, but your mortgage balance is only $300,000. You can refinance your loan with your current mortgage holder or another lender for $500,000 and receive $200,000 ($500,000 minus $300,000) once the process is completed. Your mortgage payments on the refinanced property will probably increase (unless the old interest rate was substantially higher than the new rate) because the balance of the loan has increased by $200,000, but you'll have the extra funds to buy another cash flow positive property. There are closing, legal, and other costs associated with the refinancing that you must consider when evaluating this option compared with the alternatives.

Savings

If you've been able to put away some of your salary, you could always use the savings for the down payment. Stocks, bonds, trust funds, inheritances, savings accounts, and other such sources are also available for your down payment. You could always raid your retirement accounts, such as your IRAs and 401(k). This, of course, should be your last resort because you'll pay exorbitant penalties for extracting funds before you're eligible. However, self-directed IRAs now provide investors with the option of buying real estate. Your last option is to use credit cards to finance real estate acquisitions. This is rather expensive capital, considering that rates typically exceed 20 percent per annum.

Private Investors

Private investors will provide you with down payment funds; however, you'll need to give your financial backers a percentage of the deal (cash flow and/or equity). Or, you can negotiate a fixed percentage return on the borrowed funds. Some "silent" investors simply require a fixed rate of return that is commensurate with their perceived risk for the project. Private investors might be affluent neighbors, doctors, lawyers, or an elderly lady down the street. These individuals are trying to diversify their investments, yet they can't perform the work required to locate, buy, and manage real estate properties. They are willing to invest in your project in return for a portion of the upside.

Friends and Family

You can always borrow the down payment funds from a family member. When working with family, you should always use a signed contract that outlines the agreement's terms and responsibilities. Once again, business is business and family is family—try to keep them separate.

Hard-Money Lenders

Hard-money lenders are in the business of lending to individuals who are desperate to obtain money but haven't been successful with the options listed previously. They will charge you an up-front fee and an interest rate that is higher than the prevailing market rates. Although these funds can be expensive, hard-money lenders do offer the unique advantage of providing the funds within a few days. You'll definitely receive the funds for your down payment, but you'll pay handsomely for the convenience.

Owners of the Property

Often times, the owner/seller of the property you are purchasing is willing to provide 5 or 10 percent of the purchase price in the form of a secured loan. You or your lawyer must negotiate the terms and rate with the owner. Banks often work with owner financing and are accustomed to working with investors who require seller financing to close a deal. You should always ask the seller if he is willing to provide financing to a prospective buyer.

Admittedly, when you first start buying investment properties, securing the funds for the down payment can be challenging. Once you've collected a small stable of income-producing properties and allowed them to appreciate in value, I assure you that securing the funds required to buy more properties becomes significantly easier. You'll be able to extract the equity from your portfolio and use it to buy more apartment buildings.

You should attempt to keep your day job for a minimum of two years while managing your landlord duties. Try not to leave your day job too soon, because many traditional lenders will not lend to you if you can't show a track record of more than 24 months. Once you have two years of rental receipts, lenders are more willing to work with you on a "no-income-verification" basis. Most self-employed individuals (i.e., landlords and investors) use these types of loans because they don't have a regular paycheck that shows a steady stream of income. Once you leave your day job, the no-income-verification loan (also known as a no-doc loan) is your key to the Promised Land. As a rental property owner, you may be generating a healthy income, but after depreciation and business expenses, you may show only a very small taxable profit. A no-income-verification loan allows you, the borrower, to apply for a mortgage without your income being a factor. Your LTV might be lower and the interest rate might be a bit higher with a no-doc loan, but you'll be able to secure the funds needed to close on your next property without having to show a paycheck from your 9-to-5 job.

Banking Relationship

Developing a good relationship with a local bank can be extremely advantageous. Most banks offer special programs for their premier customers. One becomes a premier customer at a financial institution by maintaining significant balances, depositing funds regularly, and cultivating a long-term, mutually beneficial relationship there. Once trust has been established, you will be able to contact the vice president of lending at your bank to discuss your financing requirements over a leisurely lunch or a game of golf. This personal relationship will make your loan process much easier and should significantly expedite matters. Moreover, local banks want to invest in their own backyards, so search for banks that are based in your target neighborhoods.

Credit Score

Your credit score is an important factor that most banks use to estimate your ability to repay a loan. It is a measurement that is determined by your timely or untimely payments to creditors, your credit/debt ratios, and your outstanding debt risk. A mathematical model is used to generate credit scores between 200 and 800. A score above 680 is considered quite good and above 720 is very good.

Having a stellar credit score indicates your ability and tendency to pay your debts on time. If you've been financially responsible, your credit-worthiness will earn you a high credit score. Banks prefer lending to investors with good financial track records, even if they don't have much experience as real estate investors. Lenders realize that good creditors have borrowed money in the past and have made repayment of it a priority. Therefore, an individual with a high credit score is less likely to default on the loan because of his proven history of paying his debts in a timely manner.

Financing and Cash Flow

Mortgage financing and the amount of the down payment can determine whether a property generates a positive cash flow each month. Consider the following comparison of two financing scenarios for the same property. Although you won't buy a condo for cash flow purposes, this example assumes a property purchase price of $200,000 and monthly rental income of $1,500.

Property Financing Scenario 1

The owner obtains 100 percent financing and secures a 30-year loan at 7 percent with monthly payments of $1,331. Add $400 for taxes, maintenance, and repairs, and the monthly payment rises to $1,731. Because the monthly rental income is only $1,500, the property will have a loss, or negative monthly cash flow, of $231. This is the owner's out-of-pocket expense needed to carry the property each month.

Property Financing Scenario 2

The owner obtains 90 percent financing (putting 10 percent down with a mortgage of $180,000) and obtains a 30-year loan at 5.5 percent with monthly payments of roughly $1,022.02. Add $400 for expenses, and this property generates $77.98 in positive monthly cash flow. It certainly does not have a negative cash flow, and the owner pays absolutely nothing out of pocket each month. By putting some money down and finding a lender that was willing to offer a lower interest rate (5.5 percent versus 7 percent), the investor is able to decrease his monthly payments by $308.98.

The type of financing available is determined mainly by the loan amount, the down payment, and the creditworthiness of the borrower.

Making an Offer

If the property's structure and systems are sound, I'll submit an offer, even if my offer is substantially less than the asking price. My offer is always based on how much I feel the building is worth, and also on how little I think the seller is willing to accept to part with his property. After all, you must always remember that you're buying a building's current cash flow, and therefore you need to evaluate it for that stream of cash. Never buy on pro forma (potential future) numbers. Many brokers and property owners will attempt to take advantage of novice investors by providing financials showing what they believe the building could generate under ideal conditions. Be sure to inform the seller that your analysis is based on current, actual revenue and expenses. Thank him for the additional information, but always use actual numbers.

Although you may not be in a position to buy a property with all cash, I once had a buyer make an offer that was contingent only on an inspection. In other words, if the building passed the inspection, he would have to close on the property or risk losing his deposit. He was a confident investor who claimed to have the means to buy my property without requiring financing. I had several offers (some higher and some lower), but the lack of a mortgage contingency made his particular offer quite appealing, so he earned the right to buy the property against stiff competition. Now, when it came time for the closing, he had lined up conventional financing with a local bank and deposited only 20 percent of the purchase price at closing. He took a chance, but he ultimately won. Perhaps he had the liquid funds needed to make an all-cash purchase, or perhaps he didn't and bluffed his way through the offering in order to win the bid. I'll never know, and I don't particularly care, because he was able to close at my asking price.

In fact, many seasoned investors make all-cash purchases and then obtain conventional financing on their properties after the closing. The advantages of buying in cash are numerous. For one thing, you don't need to go through a long-drawn-out process with the bank in order to close on a property. Also, your offer is much more appealing to the seller if you don't have a mortgage contingency and can close relatively quickly (i.e., in fewer than 30 days). Reducing or eliminating the contingencies makes sellers notice your offers. The typical contingencies used these days are a property inspection and financing. If you submit your offer with these contingencies and for some reason these two criteria are not met, you have the legal right to back out of the deal, and your deposit will be returned immediately. Therefore, the risk of losing your deposit is reduced dramatically with contingencies.

The financing contingency, should you choose to use it, is extremely important and beneficial from a strategic perspective. If for one reason or another you cannot secure a loan from a lender, and therefore you cannot close, you will not be risking your entire deposit (5 to 10 percent of the purchase price). Because the bank's commitment letter is one of the final documents required before closing, this contingency also gives you ample time to back out of a deal should you not want to pursue it further.

I like to stipulate exactly how much I'm willing to deposit at the signing of the P&S (purchase and sale contract). Instead of the standard 5 to 10 percent, you may stipulate a lesser amount of money to be deposited. If a broker is involved, he will usually want you to deposit the commission (4 to 6 percent of the purchase price). However, everything is negotiable, and because this is the money you potentially risk losing and have to forgo for 30 or more days, you should attempt to make it as small an amount as possible. Some sellers may balk at a small deposit and consider it evidence that you are not committed to the property, so try to balance the pros of this strategy with the cons of potentially losing the deal.

Negotiating the Offer

Plan to tour 20 to 50 properties in any given month and make offers on as many as meet your criteria. Of these "positive cash flow" offers, perhaps one will actually be accepted. This is a numbers game, and you have to be prepared to roll up your sleeves and get a little dirty. If you tour enough properties and make enough offers, you'll eventually find a seller who is willing to part with his investment for a price that generates a positive cash flow for you. You must always negotiate from a basis of information and knowledge. Furthermore, don't get emotional about a deal. Each new property should be just a series of numbers on a spreadsheet to you. With this mindset, you'll avoid bidding wars as well as owning properties that don't meet your cash flow criteria.

The Closing Process

Between the time you make an offer and the day you close, a lengthy process will ensue. Here's an outline of what to expect:

1. Make an offer (typically good for 24 hours). You submit an offer binding check (typically either $500 or $1,000) along with the offer.
2. Negotiate the offer. Agree on the price, inspection date, P&S signing, deposit amount, bank's commitment letter date, closing date, and so on.
3. Perform an inspection of the property. This takes place within 14 days of the offer. You should hire a professional inspection company to perform this work, and you should plan to attend the inspection and walk-through of the property with the inspector. Feel free to ask questions along the way, and get answers to all of your inquiries. After attending a dozen or more of these inspections, you'll know what to look for and can eventually perform your own inspections. If substantial work is required at the property, you might want to invite your general contractor, electrician, and plumber to the walk-through. They can be helpful in providing you with estimates for repairs. The inspector's job is only to let you know what is wrong with the property, not to speculate on how much it might cost you to make repairs.
4. Punch list. If you determine that the property needs certain repairs done before you buy it, then this is your opportunity to submit a punch list to the owner. The owner can accept or reject your requests. He can also either make the repairs or provide you with an agreed-upon quantity of money (a credit at closing) to make the repairs yourself. I always request the credit at closing, because I prefer to be in charge of all repairs made at my properties. The current

owner will not care as much as you do; therefore, he won't be as vigilant as you'd be in making sure that the property is repaired to your standards.

5. Due diligence period. Review all leases, expenses, and so on for the property and review the financials to make sure that the information that was presented to you is accurate.

6. Signing the P&S. If you decide to move forward with the purchase after the due diligence period, you must submit the earnest money deposit to the escrow agent (typically the broker, if one is involved, or a lawyer) and sign the P&S.

7. You work with your lender to submit a mortgage application and secure financing.

8. The lender provides you with a finance commitment letter. This letter essentially states that you will, indeed, obtain the funds necessary to purchase the property, and that the bank's underwriter has approved you for the funds requested.

9. Final walk-through. Be sure the P&S states clearly that you can return to the property to make a final inspection 24 hours before the closing. More than 30 days can elapse between the formal inspection and the closing date. A lot can happen during this time, so you should return to the property to verify that nothing has changed. After all, once you buy the property, any new problems are yours to deal with.

10. Closing date. Always try to buy apartments one or two days after rents are collected. That way, the owner must collect all rent due and will have to pay you the majority of the month's rent at closing. You'll have extra proceeds to deposit in your bank account on day one. All parties typically meet at the buyer's attorney's office or at the local county courthouse, where the paperwork can be submitted and the transaction can be officially recorded. Be sure to review your settlement statement (also known as the HUD-1). This document states all of your closing costs and related expenses. I'd guess that 30 percent of the time there are errors in this document, so be sure to review it carefully. In fact, I always request a copy of the HUD-1 the evening before the closing so that I have ample time to make sure it is correct. The owner will need to pay the final water bill and pro-

vide a certified smoke detector inspection report from the local fire department. The lawyers will legally transfer the security deposits currently on file for existing tenants. Because this is a sensitive and potentially costly matter, let your attorney handle this with great care. Finally, don't forget to obtain the deed and keys to your new property.

Other Considerations

In addition to evaluating a property based on its current NOI and cap rate, you'll want to understand its competitiveness in the marketplace. Figures 9.3 and 9.4 show what renters really want and are willing to pay for.

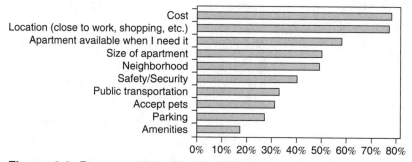

Figure 9.3 Reasons Why Renters Chose an Apartment

SOURCE: National Association of Home Builders, www.multifamilyexecutive.com, June 2005, p. 75.

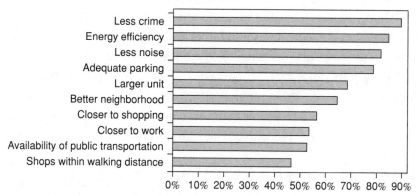

Figure 9.4 Top 10 Amenities

SOURCE: NAHB, www.multifamilyexecutive.com, June 2005, p. 76.

Economies of Scale

John D. Rockefeller Sr. said, "If you play with pennies, you make pennies. If you play with dollars, you make dollars." It is true that the bigger your apartment building is, the better the returns it will likely generate. The more units you have under one roof, the better the cash flow, and the easier it is to manage and maintain. If you want to make big money in this business, then you have to be thinking big. If you prefer playing in the little leagues for the rest of your life, then stick to single-family homes and condos. If you want to play in the minor leagues, then buy duplexes, triplexes, and fourplexes. If you want to play in the major leagues, then buy large multifamily apartment buildings. As you know, baseball players are not compensated at all for playing in the little league. They barely earn a livable wage in the minor leagues, but in the majors they can earn tens of millions of dollars each year.

Moreover, there's less competition for large multifamily buildings, and the cost per unit is less. No longer are you competing with the moms and pops of the investor world. They don't buy commercial properties. Also, if you buy buildings between 5 and, say, 200 units, you won't be competing with institutional investors, either. Buying 5- to 200-unit complexes will make you a multimillionaire. Furthermore, buildings that have more units are less prone to suffer dramatically when there are vacancies. If you own a single-family home or a condo and you have a single vacancy, 100 percent of your rental revenue is lost. When you own a triplex and have one vacancy, 33 percent of your rental revenue is lost. When you own a 50-unit property and you have one vacancy, the 2 percent hit to your revenue is much more manageable. Also, if you own a 50-unit building, it's much easier to manage, especially if you provide housing to your property manager. Find a handyman who is willing to offer his services in return for free rent. Larger buildings allow you to exchange housing for free labor without compromising your cash flow. This is simply not feasible with smaller properties.

Protecting Yourself from Lawsuits

If you know a landlord who hasn't been sued, he probably hasn't been in the business long enough. This is a prophetic statement that most experienced investors would agree with. So, how do you protect yourself from frivolous lawsuits and unscrupulous tenants trying to make a fast buck at your expense? Well, if you ask 100 attorneys and experienced investors what is the best way to protect yourself from lawsuits, you'll obtain 100 different answers. Over the years, I've received a lot of advice, but the two most frequent replies are:

1. Establish an LLC (limited liability company) and place the property in a trust with you and perhaps some family members or business partners as the beneficiaries. Should someone conduct a property search in an attempt to determine what properties you own, finding this information will be more challenging because your name won't appear on the public tax records. That said, most educated and motivated individuals could determine what you own and attempt to attach a lawsuit to your entire portfolio of real estate holdings. The property trust helps to distance you from the general public's investigative eye. It's not a silver bullet, but it certainly makes determining what you own a bit more difficult. With an LLC, properties are owned in the name of the entity, and taxes are filed separately. The cost to set up an LLC varies by state, so consider the expense and administrative burden of establishing and maintaining a formal business entity before you make a final decision.

2. Purchase the properties in your own name and carry sufficient insurance and an umbrella policy for additional coverage. This strategy will help to protect you from significant financial losses.

Be sure to ask your attorney about how to shield your personal and business assets in the event that you are sued. Based on your own needs and particular circumstances and considering all of the options available, only you can determine the best strategy for protecting your properties. Also, don't forget to file a homestead on your primary residence. The Homestead Act prevents anyone from seizing your personal home in a lawsuit.

Lessons Learned

- All banks offer different mortgage programs with varying rates and options. Be sure to compare a number of them to find the program that works best for you.

- There are many options for obtaining the funds required for the down payment that you can explore. If you don't have the proceeds in your own savings account, don't worry, because there are many choices available.
- Your credit score is very important. The higher your score, the easier it is to obtain financing at competitive rates and terms. Try to improve your credit score by paying your creditors on time and by reducing your overall debt-to-credit ratio.
- The interest rate on your mortgage can dramatically reduce the profitability of your rental property. The higher the rate is, the more you'll owe each month. Although a small increase in interest rates might not dramatically alter the monthly payments, a larger increase could reduce or eliminate your positive return.
- Lawsuits are common and are expected by real estate investors. If you plan for them and adequately protect yourself, you'll be prepared for the inevitable.
- Don't leave your day job too soon. You might not be able to secure conventional financing. Typically, banks like to know that you've been actively involved in the real estate industry for a minimum of two years. Try to maintain your day job while you acquire more properties. Be patient for a few years until you are sure that the positive cash flow from your rental properties is sufficient to pay your bills and maintain your desired lifestyle.

10

Tenants

Opportunity is missed by most people because it is dressed in overalls and looks like work.
—THOMAS EDISON

Who Rents and Why?

All kinds of people rent, and they do so for several different reasons. The most common renters include the following groups.

Transitional Renters

Renters who are in between homes because they have sold their house and are buying or building a new one are in transition. They may have recently moved to the area and need to rent until they can determine where they eventually want to buy. These tenants can certainly pay their rent, but they tend to be short-term renters. They might stay with you for a year and then leave once they've purchased their own property.

Noncommittal Renters

Renters who are not ready to buy a home may be noncommittal renters. These individuals include students or recent college graduates, low-income residents, and military personnel. They might even be professionals who have lived in the area for a long time but don't want to buy at the perceived "top" of the market. They'll wait indefinitely until they feel that the market has corrected itself—which might be a long time, depending on market forces and their own personal perception. For whatever reason, these individuals are neither ready nor willing to buy a property, yet they make excellent tenants.

Foreign Renters

First-generation immigrants tend to rent for several years until they have established themselves in the country. Generally speaking, immigrants tend to be hardworking and want to avoid confrontations with the law. They pay their rent on time, and they are outstanding long-term renters. Depending on your market and geographical area, it helps to learn a second language such as Spanish or Portuguese. In an article entitled "The Emerging Hispanic Market," *ApartmentPro* magazine (July/August 2005)

TOP HISPANIC MARKETS

City	Millions of Hispanics
Los Angeles	7.8
New York	4.3
Chicago	1.8
Miami	1.8
Houston	1.8
Dallas	1.5
San Francisco	1.5
San Antonio	1.3
Phoenix	1.2
McAllen, Texas	1.1

SOURCE: U.S. Census Bureau, 2004.

looked at demographic and housing trends for U.S. Hispanics. Its findings included the projection that by the year 2025, one out of every five individuals in the United States will speak Spanish. U.S. Hispanics total 43.5 million and represent 15 percent of the total population. Hispanics are the largest minority in the country, and this segment of the population is projected to grow by 34 percent between 2000 and 2010. According to the office of Housing and Urban Development, almost 50 percent of Hispanics rent. Nearly 70 percent of first-year Latin American immigrants rent. They tend to be unfamiliar with the procedures for buying one's own home and the benefits of ownership, and they have yet to establish the credit history necessary to obtain a mortgage. Being able to cater to and communicate with individuals from Latin American countries will be a distinct advantage for many years to come.

Section 8 Renters

These individuals receive a subsidy from the government to rent market-rate units from landlords all across the country. Many Section 8 voucher holders continue to rent because they cannot afford to buy and because this government program substantially subsidizes their monthly rental payments. Remember that there are good and bad tenants, regardless of affluence. You can't and shouldn't discriminate on the basis of a person's level or source of income. Be warned that some of the worst tenants make six-figure salaries, and some of the very best tenants make less than $30,000 a year.

Poor-Credit Renters

Individuals who have poor credit and therefore cannot buy a home tend to rent. Late payments and missed payments are obviously not desirable from a landlord's perspective, so you must be vigilant in checking a prospective tenant's credit before accepting him into your property.

Damaged-Credit Renters

Renters who have experienced a bankruptcy or some other credit problem may be trying to improve their credit. If their problems have been resolved, they could potentially be good long-term tenants. Once again, always check their credit and inquire about anything that is unacceptable.

Elderly Renters (Baby Renters)

As the baby-boom generation nears retirement age, many of them will not be able to pay for their living expenses and will opt to sell their homes and rent while living off the proceeds from the sale of their primary residence. I refer to them as "baby renters." Baby renters can be an excellent source of new tenants, but you might have to modify your units to satisfy the unique needs of an older generation.

Generation Y or the Echo Boomers (the Offspring of the Baby Boomers)

This generation is nearly the same size as the baby-boom generation (approximately 80 million strong). Children born roughly between 1977 and 2000 make up the Generation Y (Gen Y) demographic. Their average age is about 16, but the oldest are 27. As the vast majority of them enter college and begin working, they will increase the demand for apartment units. Renters of this age tend to cluster in college towns and ultimately live in locations where they can find work. The Gen Y'ers prefer living in apartments that offer high-speed Internet or wireless (Wi-Fi) Internet connectivity. They are price sensitive, so they prefer paying less rent for a smaller unit rather than more rent for a larger unit. They may not even require a phone jack, because the majority of them own cell phones. Proximity to public transportation and fitness centers is a priority as well.

Vacancies

Filling a vacancy is guerrilla warfare, and you should consider any vacant unit as a direct attack on your financial prosperity. When I think about the money I lose every day when I have a vacancy, I immediately feel an urgent need to fill it For example, $1,500 per month equates to $50 per day. It's costing you $50 each day you don't fill that vacancy. If you haven't found a tenant in a week, that's $350 taken directly out of your wallet. You could have bought tickets to a very nice show, had an extravagant dinner for two, and even had some money left over.

Each and every month, a landlord must keep his properties occupied and his clients (tenants) satisfied. Vacancies can make a once-profitable property a losing proposition. You must avoid owning properties that require you to pay the mortgage out of pocket each month. Vacancies produce only anxiety, stress, and negative cash flow. Anything less than 100 percent occupancy is, indeed, an attack on your family's well-being, and you should make it a priority to deal with the situation as quickly as possible. Filling your vacancies is paramount for your success and critical to your ability to continue in this industry. When you have 0 percent vacancy, you will feel relieved because your buildings are producing at a level commensurate with their full economic potential. This, in turn, will allow you to pay their mortgages and operating expenses and do whatever you wish with the profit.

Filling Vacancies

Vacancies are without question a landlord's greatest expense. Admittedly, I initially dreaded the thought of vacancies. They would consume my time and energy while depleting my returns and reducing my cash flow. I'd be concerned that a unit would be vacant for several months and that I'd only break even or, even worse, lose money on a property. I tried not to imagine losing two or three tenants at the same time and having to pay thousands of dollars from my savings to carry a building. If you want to be successful in this business, you must know how to fill vacancies. Conquer your fear of vacant units by learning the tricks of the trade. There are traditional ways of finding tenants, and then there are the less traditional means of finding tenants. I have listed here all the methods I've used to fill vacancies over the years.

Advertise Available Units Online

More and more renters are turning to the Web to find their next apartment. This medium has and will continue to revolutionize the way in which renters find available apartments. Be sure not to ignore this powerful and extremely effective marketing medium. Some of the most popular sites to advertise your vacancies on are:

- Apartments.com
- ApartmentGuide.com
- Rent.com
- Homestore.com

- ForRent.com
- Yahoo!: Apartments for Rent
- AOL: Apartments
- Craigslist.org (listed by city)
- Online versions of local newspapers
- Your own Web site

Local Newspapers and Publications

Every city has a local paper, and these publications typically have a real estate section. Contact the paper's advertising department to list your available apartments. Include your phone number, the apartment's details, and the amount of the rent. Sometimes less information is better because your goal is to have your phone ring. Entice prospective renters with information that compels them to call you. At the minimum, all future tenants need to know is how many rooms, where, how much, and how to contact you. Try to get your ad at the top of the column. If the order is determined alphabetically, try to manipulate your ad so that it appears first. Also, place a "hook" in your ad that attracts renters. For example, "newly renovated apt" or "huge bedrooms!!" are effective, eye-catching buzzwords.

Police Officers

Provide discounts to officers. There's nothing quite like having a police car parked in front of your building every night. You'll instantly curb any crime that may occur at your property. I always contact my local law enforcement agencies when I have vacancies and offer their entire staff a 10 percent discount if they rent from me. I will go to great lengths to secure a lease with a police officer or detective. Their contribution to the safety of your properties is priceless.

Universities and Hospitals

If you have properties located near universities, you should contact each of them. Introduce yourself to the department responsible for housing and make sure the people there know that you're interested in working with them. Once they realize that you have rental properties located in close proximity to their schools, they'll consider a housing partnership.

In fact, many universities allow property owners to post information regarding available apartments on their Web site's off-campus housing billboard.

If your buildings are located near a hospital or dental or other medical office building, you should make contact with the office managers from each company to advertise your rental. Your persistence will eventually pay off in huge dividends if you make these individuals aware of your beautiful apartment that's within walking distance of their place of employment.

Flyers

Distribute flyers within a 5- to 10-mile radius of your property. Remember that most people don't want to drive more than 15 miles to work. Bookstores and grocery stores have bulletin boards that provide space for flyers. Use them to market your vacancies.

Friends, Colleagues, and Acquaintances

Everyone you know should be made aware of your current or upcoming vacancy. I rented an apartment to my insurance agent after speaking with her about the building's policy for the coming year. I mentioned that a unit had just become available and that I was in the midst of finding a new tenant. She expressed interest, so I had several photos e-mailed to her. She toured the property the very next day and gave notice to her current landlord that evening. The moral of the story is: don't leave any rock unturned. Make everyone within your personal and business circles know that you have a vacancy and that you are eager to fill it as soon as possible. You'll be surprised to learn just how many of your acquaintances or friends of friends want to move, upgrade their apartment, or simply live in a different place.

Section 8–Local Housing Authority Rental Lists

Each of the public housing agencies that distributes Section 8 vouchers generates a list of available units for its respective towns and provides this information to individuals searching for housing. Be sure to contact the person who manages this list and request that the address and description of your property and your contact information be included.

Section 8–Inspectors

The housing inspectors for the Section 8 program view several properties each and every day. They know exactly which apartments are good and which are in need of serious repair. They know if tenants are clean and take good care of their apartments or if they live in squalor. Inspectors are a terrific source of new tenants and serve as a filter for selecting the best tenants.

Postal Delivery Personnel

Who sees more potential tenants and properties than anyone else? Postal delivery agents, of course. One agent might deliver mail to as many as 200 houses each and every day, and might even speak with various tenants along his route. These agents might know that a renter is not pleased with his current apartment and is considering relocation—perhaps to your apartment. You should consider compensating the postal agent 10 percent of the monthly rent as a referral fee. When anyone provides you and your business with a valuable service, it is good business practice to compensate that person for helping you achieve your objectives. Providing appropriate incentives is a cost of doing business that you should seriously consider. Examples of noncash incentives include restaurant gift certificates, baseball game tickets, or books.

Current Tenants

If vacancies exist, offer your current tenants a referral fee (10 to 20 percent of the monthly rent) for introducing you to new tenants. If they themselves are good tenants, they generally tend to associate with other good people. I have found more tenants through word of mouth than through any other form of advertising. If you manage your properties well, address concerns immediately, and act in a professional, courteous, and business-like manner with your tenants, no one is going to want to leave your apartments. And, they will introduce you to their friends and family who might be looking for a new place to live. Filling a building (different units) with family members tends to reduce problems between tenants and can ultimately increase tenant satisfaction and security. Family members might have their issues from time to time; however, they tend to resolve their problems amicably and faster than complete strangers.

Military

If you happen to live in an area where the military has a significant presence, you'll find that people in the armed services can be some of your very best tenants. You should contact the local military housing office and let the housing coordinator know that you have rental properties. Offer your housing to the military personnel who can live off the base. First, you'll need to complete the requisite paperwork. Then, the military will send a representative to inspect your properties to verify that they meet its requirements. Because this is a source of tenants that most landlords do not actively pursue, you might not have too much competition.

Nonprofits

Many nonprofits are in the business of helping homeless families, battered women, or families in transition. Frequently, these nonprofit agencies will rent an apartment directly from you and will be responsible for any damage to your unit. They will sign the lease on behalf of the actual tenants and assume full responsibility. Most cities and towns have multiple agencies that help people in need. Establish a working relationship with these organizations and let them know that you'd like to work with them.

How to Prepare an Apartment for Showing

Renting a unit requires much more strategic planning than you might think. You must prepare an apartment so that it is well received by prospective tenants. If you don't take the extra steps required to make an apartment shine, then you might have to wait a long time before you fill the vacancy. Follow these steps to ensure a short vacancy period:

- When you're on the phone with a person who is interested in your rental unit, try to repeat his name three or more times during the conversation. Doing this helps to establish rapport and trust.
- Try to schedule a showing the same day that the individual contacts you, or the very next day. The longer you wait, the more likely it is that the person will find another apartment.
- When making appointments to show a unit, try to make three or more appointments at the same time. Competition is good! You

could even bring a friend along who could appear to be an interested tenant. If someone senses that the unit is in great demand, she's likely to act more quickly to complete an application.

- Make sure the apartment looks good. Paint the walls; clean the floors; open the blinds and let the light shine into the unit. First impressions are critical, and you want to highlight the unit's best features. It's the equivalent of cleaning a car before selling it. Make the extra effort to present the property in the best possible way.

- Be sure that the exterior of your property is clean and presentable. Pick up any garbage, assemble the trash cans neatly, cut the grass, and so on. Good curb appeal is a critical component of the rental process. Prospective tenants who don't like what they see on the outside might drive right by the property without even seeing the inside. Probably one of the most important factors influencing the rental process is the initial "drive-by." The drive-by allows individuals to form their first impression of your property. Is the property aesthetically pleasing to the eye? Does it look well kept, clean, and safe? Can they imagine living there and calling it home? Statistics show that 55 percent of the people who rent apartments do so because they liked what they saw as they drove by the property. No amount of creative strategies will help you if the outside of your property is unattractive; if it doesn't have very good curb appeal, it is doomed from the very beginning. First impressions count so much, and most people want to see what's on the inside only if their perception of the outside is a positive one. Don't neglect the outside conditions. You certainly will not get a second chance to make that first impression. Spend the money and time required to create the proper appearance. Make the exterior of your property look so inviting that people will feel compelled to go inside. Once they walk into your unit and meet you or your manager face to face, your chances of a positive result will have improved dramatically.

- Know what is great about your apartment, and be sure that the prospective tenants are made aware of these amenities.

- Be sure to smile when showing an apartment. People are drawn to friendly individuals, and a simple smile can go a long way.

Tenant Application Process

(See Appendix D for sample application.)

Most landlords are aware of the national Fair Housing Act. This and similar laws prohibit discrimination on the basis of race, religion, national origin, color, gender, family status, or handicap. Some states also include income and sexual orientation in their housing laws. To obtain more information about the Fair Housing Act, go to www.hud.gov. I highly recommended that you follow the housing laws of your state and that you do not discriminate under any circumstances.

So what do you base your decision on, and can you "discriminate" for any other reasons? Landlords can discriminate for whatever reason they choose, as long as their discrimination is not based on any of the aforementioned "protected classes." However, you can choose not to rent to individuals if your reasons are justified, consistent, and based on the following criteria:

- Poor landlord references
- No landlord references
- Poor employment references
- No employment references
- Prior evictions
- Criminal record
- Not enough income to pay the rent
- Substandard credit reports and credit rating

The key is to maintain these standards for all prospective tenants and never deviate from them. You should document the reason(s) why you declined a tenant's application and place this document in a file for future reference. If you want to avoid complaints from your local Fair Housing agency, then you need to determine precisely what your standards are for renting and stick to them at all times. Once again, you must adhere to the Fair Housing Act.

Be sure to screen all applicants thoroughly. After all, these individuals will be living in your largest investment and, if you haven't hired a management company, will be in contact with you on a regular basis should they need anything. A tenant could turn into the worst nightmare of your life if you make a decision in haste. Be sure to check credit, criminal history, and personal, employment, and previous landlord references. Use this information to make an informed evaluation of the applicant. Afterward, you may use more subjective criteria to better evaluate an applicant's character. For example, did the individual complete the application form in full, and was the person's writing legible? Did the individual show up at the time designated for the property tour? Was the person polite and professional when you were speaking with him?

Although not every landlord does this, you might want to consider paying a visit to the person's current apartment before signing a lease. Tell the applicant that you need to visit her to deliver relevant paperwork. Seeing a tenant's current home is very telling and will either alarm you or provide you with peace of mind. Tenants who live in squalor now are unlikely to change their poor housekeeping habits after they move. You can always decide against renting to them should you determine that their living habits aren't acceptable. Do your homework. Take the time to complete this essential part of the rental process. You can avoid renting to undesirable candidates if you screen them properly.

Be sure to ask the following questions when interviewing prospective tenants. You can be as subtle as you want to be, but the responses often speak volumes about the type of person who might be living in one of your units.

- Ask if the individual has had any recurring problems at his current apartment. Problems that occur over and over again are typically the fault of the tenants themselves, not their landlords.
- Inquire whether or not the individual has had any problems with the current landlord and determine how any problems that arose were resolved. People always leave their apartments for a reason, and you need to learn the truth.
- Ask the individual how many people he plans to have living in the unit. Be sure to inform any prospective tenant of the acceptable occupancy level. The apartment is limited to the individuals on the lease and no one else. If anyone else is found to be staying at the apartment, it's grounds for an immediate eviction. If the applicant

intends to move five people into a two-bedroom unit, that's a problem that you want to avoid.

- Ask if the applicant needs to move immediately. If he needs an apartment in less than 30 days, he may have been evicted and be desperate to find new housing. If you call his current landlord, he might be inclined to give him a very good reference because he wants him out of his unit. Be aware of this conflict of interest, and always check references with at least the past two landlords.

- How long has the applicant lived at his current address? If he has lived there for only one year or less, you want to know why. Is he being evicted, or did something go wrong? If he has lived in his apartment for a decade and is just now leaving, then it would still be helpful to determine why he is searching for a new home so that you can avoid the same problems that are forcing him to move.

- How long does the applicant anticipate staying in his next place? If the response is 12 months, you know it's a short-term renter.

- Does he have a waterbed, dogs, or cats? If you prefer not to rent to families with pets or waterbeds, then you may reject these tenants.

- Does he smoke? If he admits to smoking and you prefer nonsmokers, then you may reject the application.

- Does he own a vacuum cleaner? How would he rate his cleaning habits, on a scale from 1 to 10? You may want to avoid renting to slobs who won't take care of your property.

- Inquire which features the applicant likes most about his current apartment. This helps you to keep up to date with apartment trends.

- If the individual or family is not interested in your unit, ask if he knows anyone else who is looking for an apartment. Even though your apartment might not be the perfect match for that particular individual, perhaps he has a friend who would be extremely pleased with your unit.

After a prospective tenant completes the application and you have conducted an interview, walk with him to his car. If the car is filled with junk and debris, it's a very good indicator of how he will care for his apartment.

Avoid No Shows

When you're making appointments to show a unit, it's advantageous to schedule them at the same time or at 15-minute intervals. By seeing a steady flow of renters tour your property, any prospective tenants will realize that there's ample demand for your apartment, and that sense of urgency might be needed to get a lease signed. Also, by scheduling multiple showings at the same time, you reduce the chance of driving all the way down to your property, only to find that the individual or family could not make the appointment. In my experience, this happens about 20 percent of the time.

Another way to avoid "no shows" is to ask each person for his cell phone number and to have him call you one hour before the scheduled showing. After all, you don't necessarily want to rent to someone who doesn't fulfill his promise to call you at a specific time. You can also call him on his cell phone to confirm the meeting. By scheduling multiple meetings at the same time, you maximize your chances of renting the unit.

Some individuals fill out an application because they feel obligated to do so after you've given them a tour, even though they have absolutely no intention of renting your place. To avoid wasting your time, you should request a $20 application fee for the cost of the credit check (be sure to check the local laws in your state to verify the legality of doing this). Very few people will commit even a small amount of money (for example, $20) if they really don't want your apartment. Charging a small application fee eliminates tire kickers. You can always return the fee if you decide not to rent to them.

Always leave a voice-mail message on your phone that adds value. Be sure to describe the apartment, the number of rooms, the amenities, the property address, and the price, and always request that applicants leave you a number where you can contact them to schedule a tour of the unit.

If less than 50 percent of the individuals touring your apartment don't complete a rental application, then you're doing something wrong. Someone else should be showing your units.

Try New Approaches

Too many inexperienced investors view filling vacancies as a headache or an inconvenience. Admittedly, it's time-consuming, and it can be challenging at times; however, you must recognize it for the opportunity it presents. You can upgrade the quality of your tenants and increase your income by raising the rent. You are limited only by your own creativity when filling vacancies. Make the process fun and more exciting by trying all or some of these approaches. Always remember that your tenants pay your rents, which pay your mortgages, expenses, and salary. And this is what creates the positive cash flow that allows you to live in the style that you've grown accustomed to. Tenants are your clients, and they must be your top priority.

Tenant Property Managers

Having quality tenants in your buildings is a priority. However, tenants who pay their rent on time, don't cause any trouble, don't complain, and help manage your property are worth their weight in gold.

Many of my tenants assist me with the day-to-day maintenance of my properties. Some of these activities include landscaping, painting, and trash and snow removal, as well as general upkeep. It is very common and acceptable practice for landlords to offer their tenants a rent discount for performing weekly or monthly tasks. However, when my tenants perform these tasks, I prefer to compensate them for their time. I'll pay my tenants at the end of the month for all the work they've performed. That way, if they don't do the work or don't do it properly, I can withhold their payments. If you reduce the tenant's rent by the amount you'd otherwise compensate him for his time, you can run into very serious problems. Should the tenant decide not to perform the work, you must accept the reduced rent previously negotiated, and you will also have to pay someone else to do the work. Always pay tenants separately, and do not discount their monthly rent. The tenants who do perform some tasks at my properties call me at the beginning of each month inquiring about their payment. However, they don't dare call me if they haven't sent their own rent check out or if they didn't do the work I had requested.

If you pay your tenant more than $600 in any calendar year, then you must be sure to send him IRS form 1099 for tax purposes. Also, speak to your insurance representative about the need to have worker's compensation and liability insurance if tenants are performing tasks at your properties.

If the trash needs to be taken out (trash removal is the landlord's responsibility for a building with three or more units), I'd rather pay a responsible tenant to do it than pay another individual who has absolutely no affiliation with the building. If another tenant complains about the trash building up by the side of the yard, he knows that the person in charge of trash removal is his neighbor, so he's more apt to knock on his door before calling me.

Moreover, the tenants who agree to assist you will typically perform the work for a fraction of the cost you'd pay a professional vendor. By contracting with a tenant to assist you with a property, you are instilling a sense of pride in that person—a sense of pride that the average renter never experiences when renting a property in which he has no vested interest. He will surely respond in kind whenever something or someone mistreats the property that he is diligently helping to maintain.

You need a watchdog at each of your properties, so it's a very good idea to establish a working relationship with at least one tenant. You'll compensate him for his time, but it's well worth the modest expense if he is inclined to keep your property looking good and is quick to inform you of anything that might require your immediate attention.

Know the Local Market

Accurate knowledge of current rental rates in your neighborhood is critical.

To determine whether a property is worthy of your investment dollars, you must know whether the property will generate the return that you require. You must know the property's accurate rent roll and expenses. Knowing the historical and current rents is important, but the expected potential rents are also helpful in analyzing a building's future returns. You must also know the average vacancy rate. If rents are too high, you might not be able to rent a unit for a long period of time. You'll have fewer applicants to consider and higher vacancy rates to contend with. If rents are declining, then your cash flow will suffer. Carefully tracing the advertised rents of similar units in your local newspaper and via online rental sites along with firsthand knowledge of the local market will help you to distinguish fact from fiction. Because you are buying in areas that you are familiar with, you should have a very good understanding of the acceptable range for rents.

Tenant Retention

Tenants are our customers, and they pay our salaries. They are also the ones who pay the mortgages, insurance policies, taxes, and operating expenses on our properties. We need them if we are to survive and succeed. That said, there are good tenants, and there are bad tenants. You want only the former. Good tenants are those who pay their rent on time, don't cause any problems, don't destroy your property, make you aware of anything that's gone wrong, and always obey the terms of the lease. From my experience, couples who don't have young children, don't have pets, and are away from their homes for the majority of the day because of their vocational obligations tend to be the very best tenants. Generally speaking, animals and young children cause significant damage to properties, thereby increasing your operating expenses.

Your pet policy is entirely up to you. If you have a rodent issue, then cats are the very best way to rid a property of mice and other vermin. Dogs provide a safety factor for some tenants, but otherwise don't add much value to the property unless you consider canine excrement on your lawn as adding value in the form of fertilization. Dogs tend to make a lot of noise, can be dangerous, go to the bathroom in common areas like the backyard, and destroy property. That is why so few landlords accept dogs. If the rental market is sluggish and you need to fill a vacancy, then by all means you should consider allowing pets. Otherwise, you should steer clear of them.

Compel good tenants to rent from you. Once they are renting from you, discover ways to keep them for as long as possible. Always try to retain the good ones. A good percentage of the time required to manage properties is consumed by filling vacant units. If you can retain your best tenants, you'll improve your bottom line as well as reduce your workload. If you need to paint a room or do something that you would not ordinarily do, then just do it. Finding good tenants is not easy. Hold on to them as if they were gold and keep them happy. You might spend a fortune advertising for new tenants when it would have cost you significantly less money to keep the good ones you already had. Letting good tenants move is simply bad business. Retaining good tenants is a landlord's top priority, and there are a number of ways to keep them happy:

- Offer an upgrade for every additional year that they stay with you (when they sign an extension of their lease for one year). Upgrades can be anything from painting the bedroom a color of their choosing to a one-time cleaning service paid for by management. Be sure to send tenants a small token of appreciation after they extend their lease for one year.

- Send birthday cards to tenants and offer a welcome gift package on their first day. You can determine a tenant's date of birth from the rental application and insert this information into a database that you can create at www.birthdayalarm.com. This service will send you an e-mail reminder a few days before a tenant's birthday. I certainly don't want to be a surrogate father to any of my tenants; however, I do want them to feel special and important. Ideally, I want them to realize that finding another landlord as good as I am would be difficult.

- Always make repairs on a timely basis. Fix problems immediately, address your tenants' legitimate concerns, and always be professional and courteous. Thank your good tenants for taking care of the property and for being such good caretakers of your largest investment.

- Schedule regular property inspections. This allows you to check your investment and makes your tenants feel that they are a priority. Always provide a 24 hours' notice to gain access to the property. Conduct a thorough inspection of the unit and leave a copy of the report with your tenant. If maintenance is required, then schedule a convenient time for you or your maintenance crew to return to make the repairs. Failure to make periodic inspections of your rental units, especially during the first few months of a new lease, can prove disastrous. Periodic inspections are paramount to "training" these tenants and can save you an immense amount of time, aggravation, and money. If your tenants know that you may visit from time to time (of course, with 24 hours' notice), they are likely to maintain your home better for fear of being reprimanded.

- Don't always try to maximize the rent you obtain for every unit. There's a fine balance between optimizing rental rates, thereby keeping good tenants, and avoiding high vacancy rates. If my rents are slightly lower than the average market rates, my tenants realize that they are getting a good deal and are less likely to leave. Moreover, they tend to stay at the property longer because alternative housing options aren't nearly as appealing. Reducing your turnover and keeping your best tenants, even at a lower rent, is a wise business decision. Getting and keeping great tenants is a large part of creating a successful real estate business, so do what it takes to make a decent profit while maximizing your occupancy rate.

- Some tenants can be difficult to work with. I once scheduled several repairs at a unit of mine, and I told the tenant that my handyman would be at his place by 11:00 a.m. the following day. Well, he was 15 minutes late, so the tenant berated him for 10 minutes and didn't allow access to the unit in order to make the repairs. The handyman called me and was disgusted with the tenant. The tenant called me 5 minutes later, yelling louder than the handyman. I happened to be on a train to New York City and was trying to deal with the situation from afar. I realized that my goal was to have the repairs completed in a timely and efficient manner. If I lost my patience and began to blame one party or the other, then I would jeopardize my goal of having the repairs completed by the end of the business day. Instead, I maintained my composure as both parties complained. I talked with each person to better understand the situation. I allowed each of them to vent for 10 minutes and then apologized to each of them separately. I told both of them that I really needed to have the repairs done that day and that I felt horrible about the miscommunication. I accepted full responsibility for the problems and asked that they work with me through this difficult situation. Needless to say, the repairs were made later that day. Do what has to be done to get the job done. These are your properties, and you need to assume full responsibility for everything that occurs. As a landlord, you must always be in control. Apologizing for the actions of others is the norm, not the exception. That said, while you want to work well with your tenants and vendors, you don't want them to take advantage of you. There's a delicate balance between being apologetic for other people's actions and having others abuse you for your kindness. You must learn the difference between the two to flourish in this line of work. Tenants and even vendors need to feel that you are actively listening to their concerns—that their opinion matters.

Keeping Your Distance

It's highly recommended that you avoid having a personal relationship with your tenants. That means no fraternizing, no dinners with the family, and no sharing of personal information. Accepting late rent payments cannot be tolerated, even if your tenant thinks you're his good friend. If you want to stay in business, remember that business is business and friendship is friendship. Keep it that way. Consider introducing yourself as the property manager rather than the owner. This will allow you to be the bad cop when you need to be without alienating yourself from your tenants when you need to enforce the rules. As the property manager, you are just following company procedures being dictated by the owner. Disciplinary action is much easier to accept from an employer doing his job than from a landlord attempting to maintain control.

Tenant Mix

As a landlord and real estate investor, you must know who your target market is and how to reach it. Mixing "baby renters" with college students might not be the most optimal tenant mix for all the individuals living under that roof. College kids might want to hold parties late into the evening, while "baby renters" might prefer to be in bed by 9 p.m. The wrong tenant mix will cause a great deal of anxiety for everyone involved. That said, learning the best practices of the landlord business is crucial. You will save time, money, and aggravation when you have a clear plan in place for dealing with and selecting tenants.

Rents

I prefer using a carrot rather than a stick to obtain rents on time. Late rental collection can pose challenges from time to time. If I receive the rent and the envelope is postmarked by the second day of the month, then I might consider sending the tenant a $5-10 bonus for paying on time. You wouldn't believe how many people pay on time if they can earn a few dollars. It's a simple strategy, but one that works.

If your tenants are amenable to using the electronic funds transfer system (EFT), then by all means you should encourage them to pay their rent this way. Your bank can withdraw the rent directly from your tenant's bank account if the tenant signs the requisite banking forms. This tactic guarantees timely rental payments as long as the tenant has sufficient funds in his account. Alternatively, you can save time and aggravation by opening a lockbox at your bank and directing your tenants to send their checks directly to your bank's lockbox address. The bank will then deposit the rents and credit your account immediately. You'll avoid having to make several trips to the bank to make all those deposits. You can verify deposits by going online. Time is money, and you need to maximize your available time to look for more profitable deals.

Record Keeping

Keeping detailed records on your real estate business is absolutely necessary. You are jeopardizing your business and risking an expensive lawsuit if you don't keep accurate files. A computer program like QuickBooks or Quicken's Rental Property Manager (geared to landlords with 100 or fewer units—www.rental-property-manager.com) can keep good track of all your financial information, including:

- Rental revenue
- Other revenue, such as washer/dryer revenue, parking rental revenue, and so on
- Operating expenses
- Mortgage debt
- Profit or loss per property (overall portfolio performance and individual property performance)
- Net worth

At the end of each year, you should review your annual balance sheet (a report showing your financial position at a single point in time). On a regular basis, you should review your income statement and cash flow analysis. An income statement or profit and loss (P&L) statement will summarize your company's income and expenses in detail. The cash flow statement will show you how much money you are bringing in or how much you are paying out for each property. These two statements will help you to make corrections and adjustments where necessary to improve your business's bottom line. Your accountant can create these documents, or you can generate them with the proper financial software.

Use an Excel spreadsheet or a similar program to track the following:

- Tenant inquiries, complaints, requests for repairs, and so on
- A maintenance log of the work you performed, when you did it, and what it cost to make the repairs
- Tenant security deposit account information
- Dates of signed leases and lease expirations
- Move-in and move-out dates
- Taxes and insurance (year to year)
- Current estimated market and assessed valuations for each property
- Any other interaction (whether good or bad) with your tenants

Be sure that you track all of the items listed. You'll need to maintain a log of your expenses and chronicle all of your tenants' requests, complaints, and various communications. Every time a tenant calls to make a request or to inform you of a repair that's needed, you should note the inquiry and indicate when and how the problem was addressed. Every time a tenant calls with a problem or concern, track the call in a spreadsheet. Should you ever find yourself in a court of law, the judge will question your business acumen as a landlord. This log will serve you well. You should note the tenant who called, the date the complaint was filed, the date of the repair, who repaired the item in question, what it cost to make the repair, and what was completed. Your attention to detail is critical should you ever face a lawsuit from a tenant. Meticulous records supported by detailed receipts and files will save you from an unwarranted and expensive trial. Accurate record keeping is essential to being a good landlord. If you want to succeed in this business, you'll need to establish a system that works.

Rental income and expenses are reported on Schedule E of your income taxes. The net gain or loss from rental properties is carried over to Form 1040 and added to or deducted from your gross income. You must keep a clear record of your financials, and all your receipts must be verifiable should you be audited by the IRS.

Renting to Subsidized Tenants: History of the Section 8 Program

Federal housing assistance programs began during the Great Depression to better deal with the country's growing housing crisis. In the 1970s, Congress passed the Housing and Community Development Act of 1974, and the Section 8 program was created from this act. Individuals who have Section 8 vouchers pay approximately 30 percent of their income toward their rent, while the government pays the balance. Eligible families with vouchers find and lease market-rate apartments and pay market-rate rents. The public housing agency (PHA) or local housing authority administers the program at the local level (the Department of Housing and Urban Development [HUD] administers it at the federal level) and pays the landlord the government's portion of the rent. The FMR (fair market rent) is determined by HUD. FMRs are typically based on the number of rooms in a unit as well as on the unit's location, condition, and amenities.

Who's on Section 8?

According to HUD,

- The Section 8 program provides funding for about 2 million families throughout the country.
- Of these families, approximately 60 percent are families with children, 15 percent are elderly, and 13 percent are disabled.
- Of these families, 46 percent have wage income, 36 percent receive public assistance, and 20 percent receive social security or pensions.
- They are approximately 40 percent white, 41 percent African American, and 16 percent Latino.
- The average annual income is $14,657 for families with wage income and $9,654 for families on assistance.

The Section 8 program is the federal government's attempt at assisting very-low-income families, the elderly, and the disabled with affordable housing. This government program has its unique advantages and disadvantages for landlords. As a property owner, you cannot discriminate against voucher holders, but you should educate yourself about the program regardless of whether or not you currently have tenants with vouchers.

As the guidelines stipulate, 30 percent of a voucher holder's salary is applied to the fair market rent, and the government pays the balance. As an example, let's take a family that earns $1,000 per month and has a voucher for a three-bedroom unit. Thirty percent of $1,000 is $300. The tenant would pay $300 of the rent, and the government would pay the balance directly to the landlord. If the fair market rent for your three-bedroom unit were $1,500, then you'd receive a check at the beginning of each month from the local housing authority for $1,200 and another check from the tenant for $300.

The most obvious advantage of working with tenants who have Section 8 vouchers is that the rent (or a significant portion of the rent) is guaranteed by the government. I always tell my colleagues that if I don't receive the rent check from the housing authority, then the U.S. government is in default, and I have much more reason to be concerned. The real rental risk is limited to the tenant's portion of the rent. Obviously, there's absolutely no guarantee that the tenant will pay the rent; however, you'd be assuming this risk with or without this program in place. If the tenant decides not to pay his rent, he can be evicted, and also risks losing his voucher. Because vouchers are extremely valuable and hard to come by, most tenants won't make this fatal mistake. They tend to pay their portion of the rent on time and in full.

The disadvantages and regulatory burdens are numerous, but at times they may be outweighed by the guarantee of rents. You be the judge. If you accept a Section 8 participant as a tenant, you must learn how to navigate the bureaucratic system that governs the program. The paperwork alone can create costly delays and tends to be extremely time-consuming.

After you accept a tenant based on his application, the housing authority must inspect the unit. The unit must be completely vacant. If anything needs to be corrected, the housing agency will inform you of this, and you must make the repairs. After the repairs have been made, you'll schedule another inspection. Assuming that the unit passes the second inspection, you must wait between 30 and 45 days before the new tenant can move into your unit. This can be problematic for obvious reasons. It's one of the greatest complaints I have with the system, because a market renter could move in immediately, whereas a Section 8 tenant doesn't begin paying rent for another month.

After the unit passes the inspection, you and the tenant must sign the approved lease. The lease is good for one year. You must collect the security deposit and the last month's rent directly from the tenant. The Section 8 program does not pay these fees. It will pay only the first month's rent and all subsequent rent while the tenant is living in your apartment. (For an overview of responsibilities in the Section 8 program, see Figure 10.1.)

Here are some rules that you should be aware of should you rent a unit to a Section 8 voucher holder:

1. You should be prepared to wait at least a month after the initial inspection before the tenant actually moves into your unit. Local housing authorities may require that voucher holders wait 30 to 45 days after your unit has been inspected before moving into your unit. This allows the tenant to provide proper notice to his current landlord.

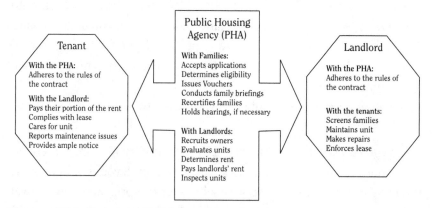

Figure 10.1 Responsibilities under Section 8

SOURCE: Nan McKay and Associates, www.nanmckay.com.

2. Your apartment is reinspected by the local housing authority every year. If anything needs to be repaired, you must correct all violations before the next inspection (30 days later), or the housing authority has the right to stop rental payments until the repairs have been made.

3. The tenant is required to provide access to the unit for the housing inspector. If he fails to provide access two consecutive times, the local housing authority can propose the termination of his voucher (depending on the specific circumstances).

4. If the tenant damages your unit and the cost to make the repairs exceeds the funds in the security deposit, the local housing authority is not liable for the damages and will not compensate you on behalf of the tenant.

5. After the first year of occupancy, the lease self-extends to become a tenancy at will. The tenant may vacate the premises after giving you 30 days' notice.

6. You are not allowed to enter into a fixed-term lease after the first year of tenancy.

7. If the local housing agency and HUD decide that the fair market rents in your area have declined, they have the right to reduce your rents immediately.

8. After the annual inspection, if the housing inspector submits to you in writing items that need to be corrected, you have 30 days to make the corrections. The reinspection will take place the following month. If the agency finds any new violations, it will warn you of these issues and return in 30 days for a third inspection. If you fail to make repairs to the items listed in the first report, it has the right to cancel rental payments.

9. Even if a Section 8 tenant signs your lease, the local housing authority's lease supersedes yours.

As you can see, the rental process, procedures, and management are much more demanding if you work with a Section 8 voucher holder, but it may be worth it. Educating yourself about the pros and cons as well as the associated legal issues is helpful in deciding how to best work with voucher holders.

HUD establishes the fair market rent on an annual basis. The local housing agencies have the right to reduce the rents if they determine that market rents have decreased over time. They are also obligated to increase the rents, but they tend to do this at a slower pace than the market. I know of several large companies with thousands of rental units that no longer want to accept Section 8 voucher holders because the uncertainty and fluctuation of the rental revenue puts them in a precarious financial position. The sudden reduction in rent would jeopardize their business, so they try to avoid Section 8 tenants (note that this is not legal).

That said, a good percentage of my tenants have Section 8 vouchers. I've had a very positive experience with this program and would highly recommend it. At the end of the day, you must perform a detailed tenant background check and must feel comfortable renting to the person or family applying for your apartment. Regardless of where the rent is coming from, you should feel confident that the tenant(s) meets your requirements.

Lessons Learned

- Don't let good tenants leave.
- Provide incentives to your best tenants so that they are content.
- Conduct thorough background checks on all your prospective tenants before signing a lease with them.
- Deal with vacancies immediately. Reduce your vacancy rate by employing all of the strategies outlined in this chapter.
- The Section 8 program can be administratively burdensome, but the guarantee of the rents can work in your favor.

11

Basic Tenant–Landlord Law

America: where there are ten million laws to enforce Ten Commandments.

—UNKNOWN

If you've thought about being a real estate investor, then you've probably imagined the ease with which you would buy a rental property, make the necessary renovations, find the ideal tenants, and then collect all the rent on the first of each month. It's not rocket science, yet it's an extremely lucrative business, right? You may not have given too much thought to the laws that govern landlord–tenant relationship.* Most landlords are law-abiding citizens who are determined to provide clean, safe housing at a fair price. What they may not realize is that the landlord business is riddled with laws that can financially and emotionally destroy anyone who fails to educate himself properly. Smart landlords

---

* Sources for this chapter: Consumer Affairs and Business Regulation, Massachusetts Office of Consumer and Business Regulation, "Landlord Rights and Responsibilities." Basic Landlord/Tenant Law for the Small Property Owner, by Adams and Sammon, Counsellors at Law.

know precisely what their obligations and legal rights are at all times. If they don't happen to know their rights, they consult with a competent attorney who will provide them with the best possible guidance. Because learning these laws "on the go" can lead to your swift demise and/or bankruptcy in this trade, it's wise to read this chapter very carefully and be sure to hire a very astute attorney. Once you know the rules of the game, you'll be better equipped to handle all of the challenges that lie ahead.

The majority of my tenants are very pleasant individuals to whom I enjoy renting properties. Eventually, however, you will rent a unit to a difficult tenant, or, perhaps, a good tenant will suddenly turn bad. You need to know how to protect yourself and limit your losses. Your tenants are important clients and must be treated in a professional manner. You can't afford to let down your guard and become close friends with them. As mentioned in the previous chapter, you must keep very precise records of your interactions with everyone who rents from you. Keep a folder on each tenant, and be sure to update the file every time there is a new complaint and/or interaction between the two of you. Be sure to keep a copy of each tenant's rental application, lease, security deposit, and any other type of document that you deem important. If you should ever find yourself in front of a judge, you'll be asked for all of the documentation you have, and your chances of winning a case will improve dramatically if you have ample, accurate records.

Avoid the urge to greet your tenants with a hug or to display anything but a professional persona in front of them. This is your business, and it is your livelihood. If you wouldn't do it in the corporate world, then you shouldn't do it with your rental business. In other words, do not act in any way that could be construed as being unprofessional. By all means, you should be courteous and friendly with your tenants, but always know where to draw the line. Avoid having your tenants take you to court, and, by all means, try to avoid having to take them to court. Lawsuits and evictions consume a great deal of time and money—luxuries that you, as a small landlord, don't have in ample supply. If you are a "people person" and don't usually have problems getting along with others, then be sure you are able to cultivate the appropriate type of relationship with your tenants.

From the very first moment you introduce yourself to a prospective tenant until the day that tenant leaves your property (of his own volition or by eviction), you must adhere to all the tenant–landlord laws. These laws are numerous, change from state to state, and could easily fill a book twice the size of the one you're currently reading. I've attempted to summarize the most important legal guidelines in the following pages.

Finder's Fee

You cannot charge a finder's fee to prospective tenants if you are the landlord and/or the property owner. Only licensed real estate brokers and salespeople can legally charge this fee.

Discrimination

The Civil Rights Act (CRA) of 1968 is commonly known as the Fair Housing Act. The CRA protects certain classes of people from being discriminated against for housing purposes. As mentioned in the previous chapter, you must not discriminate against anyone for the following reasons: race, religion, color, national origin, gender, age, marital status, handicap, source of income, and children. Write down your acceptable criteria for all new tenants and enforce these rules with every applicant. Credit score, income, employment and landlord references, criminal history, and so on are all factors that only you as the landlord can measure and score. If you don't waver from these standards and you meticulously document the reasons why you rejected or accepted particular applicants, then you should never have a problem with allegations of discrimination. If you work with a rental agent or property manager, be sure that person knows the laws so that you aren't part of a discrimination lawsuit.

Tenant Screening

You are encouraged and permitted to perform background checks on all prospective tenants. You may verify their credit ratings, prior rental history, employment, salary, criminal activity, and previous landlord references. You should have each prospective tenant complete a rental application (see Appendix D for a sample form) to determine if she meets your standards.

Have her sign the part of the lease that provides you with authorization to verify her credit and criminal history. Also, be sure to inspect a copy of the tenant's driver's license so that you can match her personal information with a legal document. Generally speaking, no more than 30 to 35 percent of an individual's income should be applied to rent.

Unit Preparation

After selecting a tenant and before his move-in date, you should have the local Board of Health or Inspectional Services Department (the agency responsible for apartment inspections will vary from state to state) inspect the unit and provide written documentation verifying that the unit meets all of the state safety and occupancy standards. You will be able to use this document in a court of law should you need to prove that your new tenant caused damages to your apartment that hadn't existed before his tenancy.

As another precaution, I also take pictures of my units and have the new tenants sign an apartment condition statement (see Appendix D for a sample). The apartment condition statement provides a detailed list of known damages and violations in the unit at the time the tenancy begins. I attach the color photos to the condition statement and have all new tenants sign both documents. By approving these forms, tenants are confirming that there is nothing wrong with the apartment (assuming that nothing was listed) and that the photos are accurate. Tenants will think twice about claiming that there are problems with a unit if you have proof of the unit's excellent condition before their occupancy. In fact, the apartment condition report must be given to the tenant within 10 days of your receiving the tenant's security deposit. Coincidentally, the majority of damage done to a property occurs during the moving day, so try to be on-site during this period of time. You'll avoid a significant amount of damage to your buildings if you are present during move-ins and move-outs.

Lead Paint

You are required by some state laws to provide new tenants with a Lead Law Notification form (see Appendix D for this document) that explains the dangers of lead paint. If you don't already have a certificate of de-lead compliance, then you are obligated by law (depending on the state) to de-lead your apartment should a child under the age of six reside in that property. You cannot refuse to rent to a tenant because the tenant has young children or a baby is on the way. Even if you have not de-leaded your apartment, you cannot discriminate against a family with children under the age of six.

Lead was previously used in paint, and when such paint is ingested by a child, it can cause lead poisoning. This disease can cause severe learning and behavioral disabilities, so the laws regarding this matter are very clear and unwavering (refer to the Childhood Lead Poisoning Prevention Program at www.cdc.gov or your local Board of Health for more detailed information). Landlords are even liable for injuries to children who visit the property frequently but don't live in the unit. If these visitors acquire lead poisoning, you are ultimately liable. I try to buy properties that have already been de-leaded so that the letter of compliance is provided as a condition of the closing. Otherwise, I've managed to buy properties built after 1978 (the year they stopped using lead in paint). De-leading an apartment can be extremely expensive and can take several weeks. In fact, you will be required to provide the tenant with alternative housing while the apartment is undergoing the de-leading process. Once you have completed the de-leading process, you must continuously prevent any paint from peeling off walls, ceilings, windows, or door trim to maintain compliance.

The Paper Trail

You must always document agreements and conversations between yourself and your tenants. The most important agreement is the contract that outlines the terms of the tenancy—i.e., under what conditions the tenant will be living in your unit. These terms must be clearly stated, never assumed or agreed to verbally. People have a habit of forgetting the specifics of verbal agreements, but they have no option but to remember a written agreement that they signed. Moreover, if it's not written down and agreed to by both parties (tenant and landlord), then the terms of the agreement are not enforceable in a court of law. Always get it in writing, no matter how trivial it may seem.

Advance Payments

You may request and collect only a security deposit, first and last months' rent, and the cost to install a new lock as advance payments before the move-in date. The security deposit cannot be larger than the first month's rent. You must provide receipts for any advance payments, and you must document where and when the security deposits were deposited. The laws regarding security deposits are very strict, and the penalties are enormous should you fail to do as the law states. If you are found guilty of mismanaging security deposit funds in any way, the tenant may sue you for treble (triple) damages as well as attorney's and court fees. Because security deposits must be handled very carefully, some landlords request only the first and last months' rent and do not either request or want a security deposit. Other landlords feel that the challenges associated with security deposits are manageable and that should a tenant cause damages, their only recourse is to obtain reimbursement from the tenant's security deposit. You cannot use the last month's rent to cover damages made to your property, so you need to weigh the pros and cons of the security deposit dilemma and make a decision based on your ability to abide by the strict rules versus your comfort level with not having funds dedicated to reimbursing you for property damages. See the next section for further information on security deposits.

Security Deposit

A security deposit is an advance or deposit of money used to secure the performance of the lease. If you decide to accept a security deposit, you must do the following after you receive the funds:

- Put the funds in an interest-bearing escrow account (a bank account).
- Furnish the tenant with a receipt for the deposit, along with the bank's name, location, and account number, within 30 days of receiving the money.

- Pay the tenant 5 percent interest each year or the actual amount you receive in interest if it is less than 5 percent.

Security Deposit Deductions

If the tenant vacates the property before the termination of the lease, the landlord may apply the security deposit to the unpaid portion of the rent for the remainder of the lease term. For example, if the monthly rent is $1,000 and the tenant leaves two months prior to the expiration of the tenancy, then the tenant owes you $2,000 (less the amount you collected for the last month's rent, if anything). You are entitled to the entire security deposit of $1,000. If there are additional damages to the unit, you may sue the tenant for the cost of all the damages. If you deduct for damages, you must provide the tenant with an itemized list of those damages and written evidence of all the repair costs (invoices or receipts will suffice).

You may retain all or a portion of the deposit for the following reasons:

- Rent that the tenant still owes.
- Payment for damages beyond normal wear and tear. Examples of normal wear and tear might be worn-out carpeting or marks on the walls. Things that are not considered normal wear and tear would be holes in the wall or ceiling, broken windows, or fire-damaged carpet.
- Any other part of the lease that the tenant fails to obey that damages the property or incurs a penalty fee per the lease.

You should make detailed inspections of all your units every six months to a year. I change the batteries in the smoke detectors in all of my properties after the first of the year, so I like to conduct the inspections at this point in time. After the holiday festivities have subsided, this starts the New Year off on the right foot. The purpose of the inspection is to discover problems that need repair while they are still manageable. If you have subsidized tenants, then the local housing agencies will conduct their own annual inspections and inform you if anything needs to be corrected.

Return of Security Deposit

If the tenant has not broken any of the terms of the lease and has not caused any damages beyond ordinary wear and tear, then the tenant is legally entitled to receive all of the funds held in the security deposit.

You must return the deposit money within 30 days of the termination of the tenancy to avoid risking a costly lawsuit.

Types of Tenancies

There are two types of tenancies: a tenancy for a fixed period of time (a lease) and a tenancy at will (often referred to as month-to-month).

Lease

A tenancy for a fixed term is created by a written lease, which must be signed by both the landlord and the tenant. A lease, in its generic form, is a contract stipulating that you will rent an apartment to the tenant, and that the tenant will rent it from you for a fixed term at a fixed rent. The rent cannot be increased during the term of the lease. The lease should also outline exactly what the tenant receives for the monthly rent (i.e., heat, hot water, other utilities, and so on). If you neglect to include this information in the lease, you should be prepared to assume the financial burden for all of the tenant's utilities. The term is typically for one year, although a longer period of time is acceptable. If you prefer your leases to expire during the spring or summer (the optimal time to rent an apartment in cold-weather states), then a lease can certainly be extended to accommodate your preferences. If I happen to buy a vacant building in the winter, I request that my new tenants sign a 16-month lease so that their tenancy terminates in the spring. It's much easier to rent an apartment in the Boston area when we don't have three feet of snow on the ground and a wind chill factor of −10 degrees Fahrenheit. The lease binds you as well as the tenant to the terms outlined in the agreement, so you should include any stipulations that you feel are necessary and, of course, legal. Do you accept pets? Can a tenant sublet the apartment? Are waterbeds, satellite TV, and painting of walls allowed? All of these issues should be addressed in your lease. Leave nothing to chance, because your tenant will test you, and if it's not in writing, then it can and will be done.

Tenancy at Will

A tenancy at will may be oral or written, but I recommend that you have it in writing. With this type of agreement, either party may terminate the tenancy for any reason as long as the notification is given with the appropriate amount of time (typically 30 days). Oftentimes, a tenancy at will commences automatically after a lease expires. A tenancy at will provides the landlord with a great deal of flexibility because the tenancy may be terminated within a short period of time. The disadvantage of this type of tenancy is that you can't legally bind the tenant for a long period of time. If you own properties at a time when rentals are in high demand or if you are planning to convert the units to condos, a tenancy at will makes the most sense. In a depressed rental market where the vacancy rates are high and tenants are hard to attract, leases might be the most prudent course of action.

Rent Increases

Many landlords are under the false impression that they can raise the rent at any time. Changing the rent requires an agreement between both parties. If you have a lease with your tenant, you must wait until the lease expires and have the tenant sign a new lease to increase the rent. If there is already a tenancy at will in place, then you simply provide your tenant with 30 days' notice of the rent increase. You must terminate the current tenancy and create a new lease or tenancy at will that reflects the increased rental amount. Both parties must sign the new tenancy agreement for the new rent to officially take effect.

Disabled or Handicapped Tenants

State and federal laws prohibit discrimination against tenants with disabilities. The laws require landlords to make "reasonable accommodations" for tenants who have a physical or mental impairment that substantially limits them (examples include speech impairments, visual impairments, alcoholism, mental illness, mental retardation, and AIDS). These accommodations allow handicapped individuals to better enjoy and use their housing. Typically, the individual who makes a request for an adjustment to the property must pay for the changes, but you should check the local laws in your state to verify this. For example, if a tenant uses a wheelchair, you must install a ramp because this is considered a reasonable request, but the tenant most likely has to pay for it. Even if you don't allow pets in your properties, you must make an exception for a person with a visual impairment who requires a guide dog. If you do make changes to your property, you can request that the tenant restore the property to its original condition when the tenant moves out.

Habitability

Heat and Air Conditioning

You must provide and maintain a heating system in most parts of the United States and both heating and cooling systems in southern parts of the country. Although tenants in Miami, Florida, use their heating systems about seven days of the year, a heating element still must be provided (usually a heater comes with a two-way window air-conditioning unit).

Extermination

You are responsible for maintaining the premises free of rodents, cockroaches, and insects. Hire an extermination company to perform quarterly inspections. The company will visit all of your properties on a regular basis to perform its services. This is a precautionary measure, but it's better to spend a few bucks now than to spend a lot more down the road as you attempt to deal with a pack of rats or mice in your property. Furthermore, if your annual Section 8 inspection is conducted and it lists rodent problems as an issue that needs to be addressed, then all you have to do is show the inspector proof that you have contracted with a licensed extermination company to provide its services on a quarterly basis. However, if your tenants leave food outside the refrigerator or place their garbage in receptacles without lids, the mice and/or rats will come and find it. They need very little to survive; a piece of bread can feed a mouse for a week.

Structural Elements

You must maintain in good order the foundation, floors, walls, doors, windows, ceilings, roof, staircases, porches, chimneys, and other structural elements of the dwelling.

Egress

You are required to keep all means of egress in a safe, operable condition at all times. That means that if it snows, you must clear the doorway of any snow or ice that might impede the tenants from leaving the building. If your tenants want to store their bikes or miscellaneous household goods in the hallway, you must prevent them from doing so; anything you find stored there must be removed immediately.

Garbage

With any property of three or more units, the landlord is responsible for the disposal of all garbage. You are responsible for maintaining the property free from trash. Some of my tenants like to overload their barrels, so I buy at least 30-gallon cans and request that the lids be placed on the barrels. Have you ever walked by a row of 12 trash cans on a hot summer day? Well, if the cans don't have lids on them, you'd swear that there's a dead body deteriorating in one of them. You can also receive a violation from your local inspectional services department if your trash cans don't have lids. The fines range from $25 to $100 in many areas.

Smoke Detectors

You are required to install and maintain smoke detectors. Typically, you need a smoke detector in the common areas, bedrooms, hallways, and basement. Be sure that the batteries are in good working order. If a smoke detector beeps several times, it's an indication that the battery needs to be replaced. You should test each detector as you make your regular inspections and encourage your tenants to inform you if a battery needs to be replaced.

Locks

Every entry door of the building must be capable of being reasonably secured against unlawful entry.

Repairs

All repair requests must be handled as soon as possible. If an emergency ensues (i.e., if there is no heat during the winter or there is a flood of water coming from the roof), you must make every possible effort to remedy the situation immediately. As mentioned previously, take copious notes detailing when a tenant called, and document each of the tenants' complaints or requests. Also, you should document when you corrected the problem and what was done.

Kitchens

A sink for washing dishes, a stove, and an oven are mandatory and must be provided by the property owner. Also, sufficient space for the installation of a refrigerator is required. Check your local laws to determine if you are required to provide a refrigerator. If you do provide a refrigerator, you must maintain it. I personally do not provide refrigerators because if I did and the refrigerators were to break down, I would have the responsibility and expense of repairing them. You're better off allowing the new tenant to buy his own refrigerator if, of course, the law in your particular state allows it.

Illegal Drugs

If you are aware that a tenant is involved with illegal drug–related activities, the law requires you to "take all reasonable measures" to evict the tenant as soon as you can lawfully do so. If you knowingly tolerate illegal drug activity on your premises, you may be subject to a fine and a prison sentence. Moreover, the other tenants living at the property may move out or withhold rent because of the unsafe conditions associated with drug activities.

How do you manage a drug problem? Evicting a tenant for illegal drug use or distribution requires proof that these activities are taking place on the premises. If you believe that these activities are taking place on your property, you should communicate your concerns directly to the police. They can assure your safety and obtain the evidence needed in court. Call the police immediately and inform them of the problem. This protects you as well as the other tenants. Request that the police pay a visit to the tenant's unit. This will serve as a wake-up call for your tenant, making him aware that he's under surveillance. Otherwise, it's practically impossible to generate sufficient evidence to prove drug use. You are better off managing the situation by making sure that the tenant is concerned with being caught and convincing him to leave or evicting him for some other reason.

Entering the Unit

Even though you are the landlord and the owner of the property, you do not have unlimited right of access to your units once they are leased to paying tenants. In other words, once the unit is rented, it essentially belongs to the tenant. You don't have the right to enter the tenant's home without her consent, and you must give "reasonable notice" before entering a unit. Access is provided so that you can fulfill your landlord obligations, but your right of access does not supersede the tenant's rights to privacy. The following are legitimate reasons to enter a property:

- To inspect the premises.
- To make repairs.
- To show the premises to a prospective tenant or buyer.
- To determine whether the property has been abandoned.
- If you have a court order. For example, if you have an execution from a judge following an eviction trial, your constable may enter the unit to physically remove the tenant.

Now, you might ask yourself, what is reasonable notice? Well, it all depends on the situation. If there's a water leak and the unit below is being flooded, then you may enter the unit immediately. If you need to show the unit to a prospective tenant, at least 24 hours' notice is reasonable. For nonemergency reasons such as the one just mentioned, the tenant might inform you that he prefers to be present during all tours or inspections of his unit. He may reject the times you have suggested, and he certainly has the right to decline access. As a landlord, you should request that your tenants suggest some convenient times that they will be home and try to work around their schedule. Unfortunately, if you have an uncooperative tenant, you should be prepared for delays and inconveniences. In fact, if your tenant suggests that 5 p.m. on Sunday afternoon is the best time to show the unit and you and your prospective tenant arrive at precisely 5 p.m., you still don't have the right to enter the unit unless you have authorization in writing. You might feel comfortable entering a unit if you've established a verbal agreement with the tenant allowing you to do so; however, in a court of law, such an entrance might be considered unlawful.

Evictions

When you realize that you and a problem tenant must part ways, you should act swiftly and without hesitation. The first thing you need to know about evictions is that you cannot lock a tenant out of the apartment. You cannot change the locks, put his furnishings in the street, or place a sign on the door stating that he is no longer allowed to return. If you try this tactic, you may be subject to criminal prosecution. Only a judge can order a tenant to move. Until a judge provides you with this right, the tenant can choose to remain in the apartment.

Before you can go to court, you have to send a written Notice to Quit (see Appendix D for a sample form) to terminate the tenancy. There are two types of Notices to Quit. The first is a nonpayment of rent notice, and the other is notice for anything other than nonpayment.

Notice to Quit: Nonpayment of Rent

If your tenant has failed to pay the rent, the eviction is for nonpayment. The notice stating the rent due and the number of days she has to comply (the notice period is determined by your state and local laws) must be sent to the tenant. I recommend that you have a constable deliver the Notice to Quit so that you have official proof of receipt and the tenant cannot claim that it was never delivered. The tenant always has the right to stop the eviction by paying all the rent due.

Notice to Quit: Other Kinds of Evictions
(Other Than Nonpayment of Rent)

The second type of notice is for some reason other than nonpayment of rent (drug use in the unit, prostitution being conducted from the premises, criminal activities, and so on). The Notice to Terminate Tenancy (see Appendix D for a sample) must clearly state the number of days a tenant has to deliver up possession of the premises. You may also terminate tenancy for no fault whatsoever (e.g., you want to take possession of the unit for a family member).

Summons and Complaint

After the time specified in the Notice to Quit has expired, you must serve the tenant with a Summary Process Summons and Complaint. You can obtain a copy of this form from your lawyer, a constable, or the court. This legal document lets the tenant know why he is being evicted, where and when the trial will be held, and how much you are claiming in damages to your property, if anything.

Answer

The tenant is given seven days to respond to the summons with his own counterclaims and reasons why he should not be evicted.

Discovery

If the tenant files for "discovery," the trial will automatically be postponed. Discovery is a legal request for information about your case. It usually consists of written questions or requests for you to produce certain documents. You must respond to the tenant's discovery after you receive it.

Trial

After you deliver the Notice to Quit, delivering the Summons and Complaint and potentially dealing with the Answer and Discovery may have taken several weeks. However, it's finally time for the trial. During the trial, you will spend several hours waiting for your case to be heard. Be prepared to spend the better part of the morning in the courtroom if you are representing yourself. Otherwise, be prepared to pay your lawyer for his time. The judge or clerk will call your name to determine if you and the defendant (the tenant) are present. If your tenant does not appear at the hearing, the judge will automatically rule in your favor, but the execution won't be delivered for another 10 days (depending on local laws), so the tenant is still given ample time to explain why he did not appear in court. Most of the time the default is removed, and the case goes to trial. If the landlord fails to appear in court, then the case is dismissed. If you and the tenant are both present, then the judge or his clerk will ask if you would consider mediation. Mediation is a nontrial process in which you and the tenant discuss the case in front of a mediator in hopes of resolving the dispute without having to go to trial. If you can't resolve the matter, then you must return to court and have your case heard by a judge. You should be prepared with a solid defense if you are representing yourself. If your lawyer is representing you, then make sure that he has all the papers and documents necessary to defend your position. The judge decides, based on the evidence, documentation, and arguments, who wins the trial. The decision is referred to as the Entry.

Appeal

Both the landlord and the tenant are given several days to file a Notice of Appeal if they are unsatisfied with the results of the trial.

Execution

The court will issue the Execution after the trial, assuming that there are no appeals. The Execution is an order that mandates that the tenant vacate the apartment. You should forward the Execution to a constable, who will give the tenant 48 hours' notice to vacate on his own terms. If the tenant refuses to move out, the constable will physically remove the tenant and his belongings with the assistance of a bonded and insured moving company, if necessary. Ask your lawyer for a reputable constable before contracting for these services.

In the state of Massachusetts, the tenant's possessions will be sent to a storage facility and will be released when the tenant pays the storage company its fees. The constable will charge you several hundred dollars for his services, and you'll have to pay the movers for one to three months of storage fees. These rules may differ in your state, so verify your responsibilities with your own lawyer.

It is far better to convince the tenant to move of his own accord than to pay a constable and moving company to do it for him. You might spend several thousand dollars to physically remove tenants. I have compensated tenants to get them to move out rather than deal with the lengthy process just described. Offer tenants $200 or more toward their moving expenses if they move out in 14 days. Whatever you need to do to convince them to move on their own is likely to be more advantageous financially than paying an expensive moving company to do it. Do not allow your evicted tenants to place their belongings in your basement or any other place on your property. A tenant could sue you for a lost family heirloom that he claims was in his possession before he moved. And guess who would be responsible for the missing heirloom? Yes, it would be you!

Lessons Learned

- You must always treat the security deposit with the utmost care. There are many laws that stipulate how to manage security deposits, and you must adhere to all of them:
  1. Put the security deposit in an interest-bearing bank account.
  2. Provide your tenants with a bank receipt indicating where and when the account was established.
  3. Pay interest earned on an annual basis.
  4. Use these funds only to make repairs to a unit on a tenant's departure, and be sure to document the cost of repairs and submit these expenses to the tenant.
  5. Return the funds (less costs to repair reasonable damages) within 30 days of the tenant's departure.
  6. Because the tenant can sue you for mismanagement of the security deposit and receive treble (triple) the charges, you must adhere to every law.
  7. Transfer the security deposits to the new landlord/owner should you sell the property.
- Many landlords collect only the first and last months' rent, thereby avoiding security deposit issues entirely.
- Consider forgoing the security deposit and simply taking the last month's rent to avoid treble charges for not managing the security deposit properly. Many tenants will use their security deposit as the last month's rent anyway.
- Never discriminate when selecting your tenants.
- Be sure to keep track of all these documents: rental applications, leases, apartment condition statements, and security deposit account information.
- Maintain a very professional relationship with your tenants. Avoid being too friendly.
- Immediately address requests for repairs from your tenants. Any delay in making repairs will only cost you more money.

- If a tenant does not pay rent on time, you need to warn him of this. If he doesn't pay the rent within 15 days, send him a Notice to Quit. Laws, terminology, and the eviction process differ slightly from state to state. Check with your local county courthouse for the specific process.
- Only as a last resort, use the court system to settle disputes with your tenants. Tenant–landlord laws are skewed in favor of tenants in many states, so try to make an agreement directly with your tenants before involving lawyers and judges. Tenants have access to free lawyers, but landlords must pay.
- Should you encounter significant tenant problems, get a competent lawyer to assist you. Hire a lawyer who has extensive experience and a track record with tenant-landlord cases.

12

Property Management

Brave men may not live forever, but cautious men do not live at all.

—UNKNOWN

What Is the Number One Reason Why People Do Not Invest in Rental Properties?

Of the respondents to a recent online survey, 95 percent indicated that management headaches prevented them from making the investment.

Be part of the 5 percent.

If you can deal with different personalities and are able to resolve problems, you can learn to manage tenants and succeed in this business. Even if you don't want to deal with tenants, you can always hire a property management company and have someone else do it.

Landlord Versus Real Estate Investor

In the beginning of your career as the owner of small properties, it's relatively easy to manage your modest rental property portfolio while working full time (assuming that you own fewer than 20 or 30 units). As your holdings increase, however, you may need to hire a property management company, especially if you aren't yet able to leave your day job. If you buy all of your properties in the same area or acquire one or two large buildings with many units, it is far easier to manage them. Conversely, if you own several small buildings scattered throughout different towns, be prepared for your responsibilities to be management-intensive and time-consuming.

Would you rather own 10 units under one roof or 10 units in five different properties in as many different towns? I prefer to have one roof, heating system, basement, exterior entrance, and egress, with as many units under that one roof as possible. But, when you start, you'll probably buy a few residential multifamily properties because they're easier to finance, and you'll need to learn on a smaller scale. If you buy them in the same town and close to one another, you'll be able to manage them without too much effort.

If you intend to expand your real estate holdings beyond the point where one person can do all of the work, you'll have to consider delegating the day-to-day responsibilities of managing your properties to someone else. Leaving your day job will free up some of your time to manage a growing portfolio of rental units, but once you have acquired about 20 to 30 units, it becomes increasingly difficult to be effective without hiring someone to assist you. When that day comes, you'll have made the transition from being a landlord to being a real estate investor—and it will be a very good day! I define a landlord as a person who finds properties, acquires them, and manages them each and every day. As a landlord, you'll receive all the phone calls from your tenants regarding repairs, and you'll either make the repairs yourself or hire a tradesman to do it for you. You'll schedule all property showings, fill vacancies, file paperwork, pay vendors, and find remedies to a myriad of tenant complaints and building-related problems. As an investor, you'll spend all of your time searching for the next deal, evaluating opportunities, securing financing, and negotiating deals. An investor spends more of his time building his portfolio with properties that make money and less time with toilets, water leaks, and repairs. By leaving the day-to-day minutiae of the business to someone else, you'll be able to devote all of your attention to the expansion of your real estate empire.

Property Management

Owners of investment properties often hire professional property managers to take care of their rental buildings. For a fee, a property management company will coordinate all maintenance and repairs, establish rents, negotiate leases, manage the eviction process, collect rents, field tenant complaints, and pay all the bills. It will receive all the calls from tenants, and you'll manage the managers instead of managing your tenants. You won't receive calls from tenants, you won't have to track them down for rental payments, and you won't have to call plumbers to fix leaky toilets. You must decide whether the expense of a property manager is worth the reduction in the workload and headaches from tenant issues.

Not all property managers are created equal, however. Ask other landlords or your real estate broker, lawyer, or accountant for a reliable property management company in your area. Also, check with your lawyer to determine how to avoid responsibility if your property manager does something illegal (e.g., discriminates, makes faulty repairs, and so on). Some managers take classes and/or exams and receive accreditation or licenses. Be sure the company you select is experienced and is intimately familiar with the neighborhood in which your property is located. Ideally, the organization will hold one of the two primary designations: Certified Property Manager (CPM) or Accredited Residential Manager (ARM). To receive this accreditation, the individual(s) must attend a series of classes covering every aspect of the business. The fee for such managers' services can range from 5 to 10 percent of the monthly gross rental income.

Property managers should:

- Follow instructions. (This is the most important criteria!)
- Be responsible, reliable, honest, and courteous.
- Be able to make minor repairs or know enough vendors to make them at a reasonable price.

- Be eager to work and deliver results.
- Live or work near your properties.
- Be detail-oriented.
- Be prompt for meetings, showings, and appointments.
- Have the ability to sell (to rent units).
- Be good listeners.
- Have contacts with multiple local vendors.

It's actually not a bad idea to manage your investment properties on your own for the first few years. The knowledge you'll gain is extremely valuable, and you'll be in a much better position to understand whether your buildings are being properly managed after you hire someone to perform these services for you. Moreover, you'll have a keen understanding of the costs of repairing and maintaining your properties. If your property manager is billing you twice the normal cost to make repairs, you'll know this immediately because of your previous experience. If your property management company doesn't meet your expectations or is dishonest, you can always find another one.

Managing a Property Management Company

Before you hire a property management company, you should interview at least three respected companies in your area. Measure their qualifications in the following areas:

1. Experience
2. References
3. Ability to fill vacancies
4. Certifications (CPM or ARM)
5. Personalities (do you like the person(s) who will manage your investments?)
6. Honesty
7. Charges (what you'll pay each month/year)

Upon making a decision, I negotiate a performance-based contract that will assure me of success. Have your property management company agree to be compensated based on a percentage of the proceeds that the properties generate. This way, the firm's compensation will be directly related to its ability to keep vacancies to a minimum while maximizing rents. In other words, if there are vacancies and the properties aren't generating their maximum potential revenue, the firm's compensation will be lower. Also, I prefer to offer an incentive if the NOI is maintained at a certain level. Because the NOI is based on rental revenue and operating expenses, such an incentive encourages the property management company to keep operating expenses to a minimum as well. If you compensate a company only on the basis of rental revenue, it has no incentive to keep your costs down. It might maximize your revenue, but you might still have extremely high expenses—and no profit.

Should you have Section 8 tenants, choosing a management company with in-depth experience dealing with the local public housing agencies is important. If your management company doesn't have this experience and you have several Section 8 tenants, it is better to find a company that does. You don't want a green manager learning on your dime.

Be sure the property manager obtains three quotes for any job that costs more than $1,000. Also, he should give you receipts for all expenses (no exceptions) *every* month. If you are billed for repairs, then you need to see the receipts before paying for them. If you are not able to tour the property after the repairs have been made, then ask the company to take a digital picture of the repaired item (before and after) and send it to you.

Without doubt, owning rental properties can be a rewarding business. It's a time-proven profession in which countless families have generated fortunes. But, it's not as easy as it appears. What you don't know can and will hurt you. If you aren't well versed in the skills needed to meet the challenges ahead of you, disappointment and despair can very quickly consume you. Now, before you hire a property management company, you'll be performing most of these tasks on your own. Here are some of the most common problems to expect.

Property Management Problems

Water

Once you have a property filled with good, reliable tenants, 80 percent of the problems that arise are water-related—leaking toilets, clogged toilets, bathtubs that don't drain properly, leaking pipes, faucets in disrepair, and so on. Finding a reliable plumber is your most important priority. In fact, I have three plumbers that I call on regularly. It's wise to have second- and third-string players as well as first-string players. Water-related problems won't wait if a plumber is on vacation or simply not available. These issues tend to be high-priority and require immediate attention, as tenants will certainly let you know.

If your water bill is higher than normal and you don't know why, then you should inspect all of your apartments. Perhaps one of your toilets is running uncontrollably, or there could be a leak in a water tank, or the tenants might be connecting a hose to a spigot in the basement and washing all the cars in your neighborhood. Don't be an absentee landlord. Be sure that you pay regular visits to your properties at different times of the day and week. Don't let your tenants take advantage of you if, in fact, you are not at the property regularly. I once informed my tenants that I'd be on vacation for two weeks and that they could reach me by cell phone for any emergencies. That was a mistake I'll *never* repeat. When I returned from my vacation, I received my water bill for one of my properties, and it was 150 percent higher than the average monthly bill. What on earth had happened? Well, the tenants knew precisely when I'd be gone, so they ran a hose from a basement water source and filled a several-hundred-gallon pool next door. To make matters worse, after they filled the pool, they encouraged the kids from the neighborhood to have fun with the running hose during some of the hottest days of the summer. Your tenants will abuse you, if you let them. Make sure they respect you—and certainly don't tell them when you'll be out of town. If you take vacations, then simply field any calls with your cell so that your tenants never know where you are.

Another way to reduce the water bill is to install low-flow water fixtures in the bathrooms and kitchens. They can be obtained free from your city's water and sewer commission, or you can purchase them directly from most hardware stores. These devices reduce the quantity of water that flows through the water source, and they are a fast and inexpensive solution to reducing the water usage at your property.

As my father used to say, "If you don't tell your money where to go, it will tell you where to go—and that might be to bankruptcy court!" Be sure to track both your rental revenue and any other revenue generated from your properties (including washer and dryer, parking, billboard, and storage revenue) as well as your operating and mortgage expenses (mortgages, taxes, insurance, electricity, water, garbage removal, and maintenance). You should be able to compare historical revenues and expenses by category so that you're better equipped to analyze and correct any fluctuations. As an example, I once received a water bill and entered the data into my property management program. By careful analysis, I realized that the bill was 20 percent higher than the historical average. Armed with this information, I spoke with each of the tenants in the building and conducted a thorough inspection of each unit. I discovered a toilet with a slow leak. The issue was immediately addressed, and my next water bill was back to normal.

Keys, Locks, and Doors

Make sure your lease clearly states that when a tenant loses a key, he must pay for changing the locks. You want to avoid burglaries, but the tenants must know that there are financial repercussions if they lose their keys.

I have created a master key for all of my buildings. One key opens every door in my real estate portfolio. It's the wisest investment I've ever made. Today, my property managers have one key that opens every door in each apartment. Spend the extra money and have a master key system developed for your properties.

My locksmith keeps an extra set of my tenants' keys in case they get locked out and no one is nearby to open the door. He often will meet with them to open their doors and provide another set of keys. They must pay him on the spot for this service. For added security, I had my locksmith install door closers on all of the exterior doors. That way, when someone opens the front or back door, the arms automatically close the door, and my buildings are significantly more secure.

Windows

Always install blinds in your windows. For approximately $3, you can outfit each of your windows with very nice vinyl blinds. You don't want your tenants to install their own version of window coverings (e.g., flags, newspapers, and bed sheets) in lieu of the blinds you neglected to install. If given the opportunity, your tenants can make your building look dilapidated and run down, and this will reduce the value of your property. Frugality with your expenditures is wise, but this is an expense that you must absolutely budget for.

Lightbulbs

I once had a tenant call me at 2 a.m. requesting that I replace the light in his kitchen. He claimed that the light did not work, and that this was posing a safety issue for his family. I visited the property at 6 a.m. and discovered that he simply needed a new lightbulb. Didn't he know this? Hadn't he checked the bulb? Well, this was his first apartment, and he wasn't accustomed to performing such "complex" assignments on his own. Actually, I assume full responsibility, because I should have asked him to check the lightbulb. In fact, whenever tenants call with a problem or concern, be sure to speak with them for at least five minutes to determine the source of the problem. About 50 percent of the time, I'm able to resolve matters without having to visit the property or send my handyman there. And, at $30 an hour for my handyman and $50 an hour for my plumber, that's a very productive five minutes, indeed.

The lightbulb rule is very simple: you are responsible for lightbulbs in the common areas (hallways, basement, and exterior part of the building), and your tenants are responsible for lightbulbs inside their own apartments.

Tenants Who Want Upgrades While They Are Still Living in the Units

I've had tenants request upgrades such as painting their entire apartments a different color, hardwood floors, new stoves, and so on. I try to avoid major upgrades to an apartment until the unit is vacant. That way, I don't spend a fortune on a unit only to have the tenant move out a few months later. I'll make the necessary investment if a new stove is required or if the paint is falling off the ceiling. But certain upgrades are unnecessary. For example, a tenant of mine once requested that I install hardwood floors because the carpet was worn.

I reluctantly installed the hardwood floors, and to my surprise the tenant moved out a few months later. The floors were damaged when she vacated, so I needed to spend more money to re-sand them. The moral of the story: try to delay major expenses and upgrades until the tenant actually moves out. That said, if you have an outstanding tenant whom you want to keep, and he is making a relatively minor and reasonable request, it is best to do it without question. Of course, if a request is safety-related or a potential code violation, the situation must be remedied immediately. My philosophy is to fix problems now to avoid paying much more later.

If a tenant wants to paint the unit after living there for two years, a reasonable compromise is to buy the paint and have her perform the labor. Such cooperation results in a win-win situation. If you painted the apartment recently, suggesting that the tenant wait a year is also quite reasonable. There's no need to paint twice in the same year.

Tenants who make several frivolous and expensive requests have to be managed better. They must realize that when your costs increase, the possibility that you will increase their rent to cover the costs also increases. That said, I do encourage my tenants to contact me immediately if there's a problem (e.g., a water leak, heating issues, a burglary, roof damage, a fire, and so on), but I also try to find a balance between those tenants who are high maintenance and the costs associated with their requests.

Satellite TV

You cannot prevent a cable operator from entering the building to install or maintain the cable system if one or more tenants have requested cable. However, the cable company cannot install cable on your property without your permission. That said, do not allow your tenants to install satellite TV on your building without your permission. In fact, I have a penalty clause in my lease of $200 should a satellite dish be installed without my authorization. Here's why: when a nonprofessional roofer drills holes into your roof to secure the satellite dish, a multitude of problems can arise, such as a leaking roof and significant ceiling damage. You should allow the installation of a satellite dish only on the side of the building or on a nearby pole or tree. Direct TV's policy is to make an installation only with the owner's permission; however, many tenants claim to be the owner, thus making it more difficult for the company to obey your wishes. The satellite dish installer will also run cables anywhere he likes and drill anywhere he wants to. These people don't seem to care whether the cable installation is well planned and aesthetically pleasing. You should either be there when the dish is installed or inspect the work afterward. You have the right to call the installers back to your property and request changes. You might also request some sort of compensation for allowing the company to provide service to your properties.

When Tenants Violate the Terms of the Lease

If your lease clearly states that there is no smoking, no waterbeds, no dogs, and no one allowed to reside in the property if he or she is not on the lease, then your tenants must live by those terms. They signed the contract and are aware of the lease agreement. They have a copy of the contract and can refer to it at any time. Should they choose not to obey the terms of the lease, you should first send them a warning letter. Afterward, you should have your attorney send them another letter. If they still don't comply with your requests, you can and should file for eviction. Send them a notice to stop the violations and deal with the problem legally. As a landlord, you need to always be in control of the situation. If your tenants think you're flexible with the terms of the lease and easily manipulated, they might decide to disobey all of your rules.

Damage Caused by Tenants

If you discover a hole in the wall or a door missing, then it's indeed the tenant's responsibility to pay for the repair. It's much more difficult to prove that the tenant was at fault when the damage occurred on the exterior of the building. For example, a window or screen may be broken. You will need to make these repairs and hope it doesn't happen again. But, if the damage is caused from the inside, then you should make note of the problem, fix the problem, and then submit a copy of the repair costs to the tenant. Be sure to let the tenant know that the repairs are being deducted from his security deposit. This notice will help to prevent further damage in the future.

Emergencies

There's no greater emergency than a fire. On one occasion, while I was enjoying a leisurely winter vacation, I received a call from a gentleman asking whether he could board up my building. My immediate response was, "Are you crazy? Why would I want you to do that?" He went on to explain that a fire had just ravaged my building and that it appeared to be a total loss. Fortunately, no one was hurt, but the entire building had, indeed, been destroyed by a fire that was started by one of my tenants' children. The boarding companies call you first—even before the fire department. You see, the boarding companies listen to the radio to hear where the fires are taking place. They then determine who the owner is and request permission to secure the property, board up the windows and doorways, and clean up the premises. For this service, the boarding companies are well compensated (by you!).

Afterward, you'll begin receiving calls from the public insurance adjusters. These firms can represent you to help you secure the highest possible reimbursement from your insurance company. For this work, they receive between 5 and 10 percent of the entire insurance settlement. Most landlords who have experienced a fire are proponents of using the services of insurance adjusters. If you're fortunate, you'll receive a final settlement agreement within three to six months. All of the insurance proceeds will be made out to you (or the owner of record) and your mortgage company. After you pay off the mortgage, you can use the excess funds (if there are any) to begin rebuilding. You'll probably need a construction loan if you don't have the funds for the construction phase. You should speak with a bank immediately after the fire to begin securing those funds. It's not the end of the world if you have a devastating fire in one of your rental properties. Always be sure to keep calm and never lose sight of your end goal.

Screen and Prevent Problems

The best way to avoid most unnecessary maintenance issues is to screen your tenants extremely well and know who will be renting from you. The most costly expense for any landlord is a tenant who destroys an apartment, refuses to pay rent, and delays the eviction process for many months. Don't be a victim of unscrupulous tenants who abuse the system.

How to Increase the Value of a Property through Improved Property Management Techniques

If you can buy mismanaged buildings and manage them well, there's significant value to be generated. By increasing revenues, decreasing operating expenses, and avoiding tenant turnover, you can increase the net operating income, and the value of the property will rise. Because the value of multifamily properties is determined by a very simple equation, the manipulation of the factors that positively influence this equation should be understood.

$$\text{Value of property} = \text{NOI/cap rate}$$
$$\text{NOI} = (\text{annual revenue} - \text{annual vacancy loss} - \text{annual operating expenses})$$

Let's assume that the cap rate in your area is 10 percent. The only way to increase the value of the property is to increase the NOI. As the NOI increases, the market value of your property (i.e., the price someone will pay for your property) swells. How can you do this? It's actually quite simple. Find a way to increase your rents, eliminate vacancies, and reduce the operating expenses required to maintain your property. That's the magic formula. For every $1,000 increase in the NOI, you increase the market value of your property by $10,000 ($1,000/0.10 = $10,000). If you can increase the NOI by $10,000, you'll have a property that's worth $100,000 more! You get the picture now?

Property Example
Year 1

Annual rental revenue = $400,000

Annual vacancy loss (a poorly managed building with high vacancy) = ($100,000)

Annual operating expenses = ($150,000)

$$\text{NOI} = \$400{,}000 - \$100{,}000 - \$150{,}000 = \$150{,}000$$
$$\text{Value of the property} = \$150{,}000/0.10$$
$$= \$1{,}500{,}000 \text{ (assuming a 10 percent cap rate)}$$

Year 2

After reducing operating expenses by $50,000,

$$\text{NOI} = \$400{,}000 - \$100{,}000 - \$100{,}000 = \$200{,}000$$
$$\text{Value} = \$200{,}000/0.10 = \$2{,}000{,}000$$

You've just added $500,000 to the value of the property through improved management techniques.

Now you can extract the extra $500,000 with an equity line and buy another building. By reducing your operating expenses by just $50,000, you were able to increase the value of the property by $500,000 (assuming a 10 percent cap rate). This is how the really successful investors grow their property portfolios and become rich.

Well, how can you accomplish this great feat?

1. Make property improvements that permit you to raise rents.
2. Reduce expenses by reviewing all of the maintenance expenses and analyze them for possible savings. Here's a list of the expenses to consider:

   Operating Expenses
   - Taxes
   - Insurance
   - Heat (common gas and/or oil)
   - Electricity (common public meter)
   - Snow removal and landscaping
   - Water and sewer
   - Trash removal
   - Maintenance
   - Management fee
3. Negotiate contracts with vendors to secure better deals for such things as trash pickup, snow removal, landscaping, and property management.

4. Buy frequently used items in bulk.
5. Be vigilant with water consumption, and make repairs immediately if there is ever a water leak.
6. Review your insurance policy for savings.
7. Speak with your county's tax assessor to determine if your property has been assessed too high.

You can also increase the revenue through ancillary income. If you can't raise rents any more, you can reduce the property's expenses, decrease vacancies, or increase its revenue to improve the NOI and thus the property's value.

By leveraging your relationship with third parties, you can develop a nice revenue stream that's not necessarily related to the rent but is directly related to the tenants themselves. Some third parties include companies that provide the following services to your tenants: telephone, cable, washers and dryers, high-speed Internet, parking garages, vending machines, and so on. Ancillary revenue should not be overlooked, no matter how small your building might be. Ask these vendors to compensate you for providing access to your tenants. Of course, the more properties you own, the more leverage you'll have with these vendors. A small increase in revenue can dramatically affect the NOI, so don't leave any rocks unturned in your quest to increase the NOI.

Lessons Learned

- A landlord deals with the day-to-day management of his properties. A real estate investor hires a management company to deal with these problems and devotes his time to finding more moneymaking properties.
- A property management company will charge you a percentage of the gross collected rents but will assume all of the management duties and tenant-related issues.
- Try to manage your properties in the beginning to learn as much as possible about the business. Afterward, hire a management company so that you can expand your business to the next level.

13

Contractors and Property Maintenance

Luck is not chance; it's toil. Fortune's expensive
smile is earned.

—EMILY DICKINSON

I should dedicate an entire book to this topic rather than just this one chapter. There's so much I have learned during the past few years, and I want to be sure to impart all of that knowledge to you in the coming pages. Maintaining your buildings is paramount to your success. If you are paying top dollar for repairs and renovations, you'll never make a profit. If you can't find reliable and honest tradespeople to perform the work, you'll become frustrated very quickly—and you may give up. There are a few basic rules you need to follow in order to maintain and renovate your properties properly and to keep contractors in check on projects of larger scope than a simple service call.

Rule No. 1: Don't Trust Any Service Vendor, Especially If You Don't Know Him Very Well

I once hired a general contractor (GC) who was working on a project near one of my multifamily properties. At first, he seemed knowledgeable, courteous, and professional. In fact, several of his clients provided stellar references. He seemed to be the perfect match for the assignments I required him to perform. Buyer beware: first impressions can be deceiving!

Four weeks later, I terminated my contract with this individual shortly after I realized that he was spending the majority of the day on the phone scheduling future jobs, trying to bill me for projects not completed, and invoicing me for hours never worked. To make matters worse, he was receiving kickbacks from subcontractors and was negligent in his own work. Other than that, he was a pretty nice guy.

Rule No. 2: Contractors Should Be Insured with a Workers' Compensation Policy and a Liability Policy and Pay Taxes on Earned Income

Obtain a copy of the vendor's insurance documents directly from his insurance agent rather than from him personally. Such tradespeople have been known to white-out dates and create faulty documents. This way, you don't have to worry about forged insurance papers. The vendor should also complete a Form I-9 (www.irs.gov/pub/irs-pdf/fw9.pdf) before beginning any work. Once you get the completed I-9, if the vendor earns more than $600 from you during the past year, you should send him a Form 1099 for tax purposes.

Rule No. 3: When Hiring Anyone Who Will Be Working at Your Properties, Take These Precautions

1. Make a copy of the service vendor's driver's license and note his license plate, phone, and social security numbers.
2. Contact, verify, and keep a record of the person's references.
3. Visit a job site at which the person recently completed work to examine it and speak with the property owner.

4. Be sure to put all of your requirements in writing and have the vendor sign a contract. Be sure to include the payment plan, the full scope of your project, and detailed information regarding your expectations. As someone long ago correctly stated, the devil is in the details.

5. Encourage the vendor to provide a timeline for conducting the work. Then, note this in the contract and provide incentives for finishing the work on time. Pay an extra 1 to 5 percent bonus if the job is completed in the time allotted. You can also negotiate a daily penalty if the job is not completed on time.

6. Be sure your vendor shows up at your project every day. Once the project commences, you must avoid down (nonwork) days. Often, a contractor will schedule multiple jobs and attempt to service all of them in the same workday. A schedule of one day at Matt's site, one day at Jim's property, and another day at your building simply is not going to work in your favor. This is not acceptable and will only delay your project. You must be your vendors' number one priority, and you accomplish that by inserting clauses in the contract that penalize them for this behavior.

7. All contractors must keep a clean working environment at all times. Before going home for the evening, they must clean everything. Make this a rule.

8. Solicit at least three bids for any major project. After receiving the first round of estimates, request each of the vendors to submit a best and final offer. Then, the two most competitive bidders can earn your business by competing against each other. It's not entirely out of the ordinary to receive bids in which the vendor has a markup of 100 percent or more. Do your homework; it's worth the time.

9. Be prepared to fire any vendor working for you, and have another one waiting on standby. It's much better to cut your losses than to continue working with a thief or an incompetent person, both of which you should expect to come into contact with, believe me.

10. Search your local Better Business Bureau (BBB) site to determine whether any complaints have been filed against the company you're considering. If you terminate any vendor, be sure to contact the BBB and file your own complaint so that the same problem isn't repeated.

11. Speak with your local town hall officials and inquire of the building, electric, or plumbing inspectors about the vendor's reputation. Often, the inspectors have been working in the town for several years (sometimes decades) and know the good and the bad tradespeople. They might even provide you with references, or at least steer you in the right direction.

12. If you are not satisfied with the quality of a vendor's work, you must be sure that the vendor is aware of your concerns and addresses any issue immediately. Don't be shy about telling your contractor that you prefer she do something differently. Also, you can obtain a second opinion about the best construction materials to use or ways to perform specific tasks from skilled third parties. Use this information to ensure that your contractor is performing quality work with quality materials.

13. Never pay a vendor before he starts the job. Vendors typically request between 30 and 50 percent of the total project costs in advance to pay for the materials and the first week of labor. In fact, in some states it is illegal to request more than one-third of the total project costs in advance, but some contractors will prey on those who are not informed. This is standard practice; however, I pay a maximum of one-third of the total project estimate only after the first day of work has been completed. That way, the workers have deposited the materials on my job site and have begun the project. I never pay the final amount until the job has been completed and inspected. Once you make the final payment, you lose your leverage with the vendor and risk everything. *Never*, and I repeat, *never*, make a final payment until you're absolutely satisfied with the results. If possible, hold back as much as possible until the end. The more money you have of the vendor's, the more likely it is that you'll receive what you ultimately want.

14. If you've hired hourly laborers, always be sure to provide them with a time sheet. Have them fill it out daily, and be sure to check their progress when possible. I don't recommend hiring people by the hour. It's best to negotiate a price you're comfortable with and then draft a contract. That way, you won't be disappointed if it takes

a week to paint the interior of an apartment when you thought it would take only two days. Moreover, you rarely (if ever) save money on time-and-material projects. Service vendors typically prefer to bill you on a time-and-material basis, because they know they'll make more money from you as the project is extended.

15. Negotiate as much as possible after a vendor presents his estimate. It's unusual to receive a vendor's best quote on the first proposal. In fact, it's my experience that most tradespeople inflate their price, knowing that they'll be negotiating downward later. They pad the quote in preparation for these negotiations. Don't be bashful about negotiating with firm vigor. Vendors fully expect it and will be surprised if the first proposal is accepted without some sort of bargaining.

    A good friend and fellow investor once recommended working the numbers backward after receiving an estimate. This approach allows you to negotiate from the high ground. After reviewing an estimate, ask how many laborers will be on the job and how many days it will take to complete the project. Ask the vendor to provide the actual pricing for the material. Given the hours required for the job, the number of laborers, the cost of material, and the final price, you can calculate the hourly rate you'd be paying the laborers. One vendor was attempting to charge my colleague $300 an hour for unskilled laborers. Do you know any unskilled laborers who earn as much as a downtown attorney in a prestigious law firm? When he approached the contractor with his analysis, the embarrassed vendor agreed to reduce the estimate by nearly 40 percent.

16. To avoid markups in material, I suggest that you ask the vendor to provide a materials list. After receiving it, go to your local Home Depot, Lowe's, or lumber/hardware store and ask them to deliver all of the items before the vendor begins the job. A nominal shipping fee of $50 is certainly worth the hassle and inconvenience of picking up the items yourself. You then can deduct the cost of the materials from the vendor's invoice.

17. Get a credit card that rewards you with frequent flyer miles and/or points with hotels. Use the card for your rental business, and pay

all of your vendors and material suppliers with this card. After a few years (or a few months, depending on the number of projects you have), you'll be enjoying vacations to exotic destinations without having to pay for the airfare or the hotel accommodations.

As a landlord, you'll be confronted with many day-to-day problems that must be resolved. As I already mentioned, it is your responsibility to make repairs as soon as possible. In the past month, my property managers have had to repair a broken window, fix a leaking toilet, repair a light that was inoperable, adjust a bathroom door that fell off its hinges, and unplug a toilet that wasn't flushing properly. These kinds of repairs are quite common maintenance issues, but they can be costly and will consume your time, even if you have someone else making the repairs. You could be jeopardizing your tenant's safety, and the problem could ultimately cost you more money if it is not attended to promptly, so take care of your business and your clients by making repairs immediately (as in right *now*).

One of my tenants called me when her unit's heating system stopped working. I immediately called my HVAC contractor, but he was busy with other issues and could not fix the system until that evening. I waited patiently and decided not to call another vendor. The contractor called me later that evening to inform me that he couldn't go to the property until early the next morning. By the time he called me back, it was too late to get someone else, so I had no option but to buy my tenant a few space heaters and wait until the morning. The delay was a mistake that eventually cost me $3,000! The apartment went without heat for more than 24 hours, the temperature dropped below 5 degrees, and the pipes froze. It took three plumbers more than two days to thaw out the water pipes. At $100 an hour, you can see that the decision to wait was the wrong one.

At another property, I have an electric heating system, and each of the rooms has its own thermostat. One of my tenants decided to economize during the winter, so he turned off the heat in the kitchen, and the pipes eventually froze. It was clearly the tenant's fault, so I sent him a formal letter reprimanding him for his action and sent a copy of the lease that clearly stated that the tenant must continue to heat all rooms during the winter months. I also informed him that the repairs would be paid from his security deposit, and I had him sign a letter authorizing me to deduct the expenses accordingly. I, of course, provided receipts for all of the work performed.

That said, I now send a letter to all of my tenants at the beginning of each winter, educating them about freezing pipes and the importance of heating their units properly. I also make sure that all of my units are well insulated and all of my water pipes are covered with high-grade pipe insulation. It's a small financial investment to make to avoid paying plumbers $100 an hour to thaw pipes during the winter months. You will make mistakes as a landlord, but you will learn from those mistakes and become a more astute property owner each and every year.

While out of the country for the holidays one year, I received a call from a tenant informing me of a broken window. He claimed that a child had thrown a ball through a kitchen window and had broken the glass. I had my doubts, so I investigated the situation thoroughly with an individual who repairs windows professionally. If the tenant had broken the window from the inside, it would have been his fault. The experienced window installer examined the glass more closely; he told me that the penetration actually did occur from the exterior of the building and that the frame was slightly bent from the outside. Sometimes your tenants do tell the truth, so give them the benefit of the doubt unless you can prove otherwise.

You should perform an inspection of your units every six months to a year, so that you can detect any small problems that may eventually turn into more costly headaches if they are not addressed. Property maintenance is much like having cancer: if you diagnose the symptoms early enough, you can avoid the life-threatening disease. If you have Section 8 tenants, make an inspection of the unit one to two weeks before the annual inspection, so that you can correct any problems before the local housing agency finds them.

Lessons Learned

- Verify the contact and business information for any vendor you decide to hire.
- Always sign a contract with a vendor before he begins any work. Detail all of the work to be performed, warranties, conditions,

costs, a project timetable, and a project specification list in the contract.

- Never pay for a job in full until you have inspected the final work and are satisfied with the finished product.
- The contractor must obtain all requisite permits.
- All contractors should have liability and workers' compensation insurance.

14

Your Team

Keep away from people who try to belittle your ambitions. Small people always do that, but the really great make you feel that you, too, can become great.

—Mark Twain

Needless to say, you cannot be an expert in every facet of your real estate business. You must delegate various roles and responsibilities to others who are more qualified than you to perform certain tasks. In fact, smart investors delegate many projects to others and learn techniques to best manage their team to ensure success. To achieve the highest possible productivity from your team members, you need to surround yourself with exceptional people who are capable, motivated, and dedicated to achieving your goals. With the right team players in place, the likelihood of success increases dramatically.

The Most Important Members of Your Team

The most important members of your team are an attorney, an accountant, your spouse or significant other, service-providing vendors, real estate broker(s), mortgage broker(s), a mentor, and your colleagues. It may take you several months or even years to assemble the perfect team, but you must choose these team members wisely and evaluate them regularly.

Attorney

Your lawyer must both be knowledgeable about general (civil) law and be a specialist in real estate. In fact, it's imperative that you hire an attorney who specializes in real estate and has extensive knowledge of landlord–tenant practice. He will guide you through the intricacies of dealing with tenants as well as the complexities of managing your income-producing properties. Your lawyer should educate you about the laws and shield you from lawsuits. A good lawyer will always represent your best interests. He should know what your goals are and formulate a strategy to help you reach them. Your lawyer will be invaluably instrumental in these situations:

- During the negotiation for the purchase and sale of any new properties
- At the closing for new acquisitions
- During eviction procedures
- Responding to and defending any lawsuits against you
- Providing advice or guidance for dealing with your tenants
- During the disposition of your properties

Your attorney is your confidant who knows everything about the properties you own and how you manage them. He should be qualified and experienced, and should also be someone you genuinely like. He will be privy to all of your business matters—more so than anyone else on your team. Needless to say, your lawyer is an extremely important team member, usually your team captain, so choose your counsel wisely.

Tax Accountant

Your accountant must also be experienced and should have extensive real estate knowledge. Many accountants are CPAs (certified public accountants); however, not all of them have specific experience with real estate. I hired two accountants and was disappointed for several years before finding my current tax advisor. Don't hire an accountant just because he comes highly recommended by a friend or because he prepares your personal tax returns. It's worth paying slightly more to have your taxes prepared in order to work with an individual who truly knows and understands the real estate tax code. Before you buy, and especially before you sell, call your accountant to determine the tax implications of your decisions. You need to know the best techniques for positioning your portfolio to avoid, prevent, or delay paying taxes. Don't avoid paying taxes altogether. Paying taxes is, indeed, a good thing, because when you pay them, it means that your fledging realty empire is actually *making money!* However, a good tax accountant will prevent you from paying too much to Uncle Sam when you could have legally paid significantly less. Just because the government seems to frivolously dispose of money from time to time doesn't mean that you have to as well.

Your Spouse or Significant Other

Your spouse or significant other provides your support mechanism, both at home and at work. He or she sincerely needs to believe in what you are trying to accomplish and support you in your effort to succeed. I've seen many wannabe investors refuse to get into the rewarding game of real estate investing because their spouses simply didn't share the same dream and wouldn't permit them to take the risks. Spouses and significant others can be your biggest cheerleaders or your heaviest dead weight. As noted earlier, you must surround yourself with individuals who will encourage, support, and contribute to your success, even if the contribution is merely psychological.

Vendors: Electrician, Plumber, Carpenter, Handyman

These tradespeople will assist you with the maintenance of your properties. You'll be calling them regularly to service your rental units. When a tenant calls you at 9 a.m. on a Monday morning to inform you that his toilet won't flush or her bathtub won't drain properly, you'll need to make a rapid call to a plumber to resolve this pressing issue. Make sure these vendors are reliable, honest, and experienced. You can expect to pay a plumber $50 or more an hour, but the good ones will save you large sums of money in the long run. An electrician will cost even more on an hourly basis, but the savings will be equally substantial. Establish a good working relationship with these service vendors, and they will respond to your calls quickly and make the repairs promptly, without overcharging you. You might have to try several vendors before you find the right ones, but you'll eventually find a complete team that you can rely on repeatedly. In fact, I have one primary vendor in each category (electrical, plumbing, carpentry, flooring, roofing, and so on) and several backups in case my primary vendor is on vacation or simply not available. The depth of your team is as important as the quality.

Real Estate Broker

A motivated broker who understands your goals and is willing to work with you is a vital asset to your team. Brokers understand value and are privy to valuable information. They can share opportunities with you that make good financial sense and can provide critical data (comparable sales, vacancy rates, market rents, and so on) to help you make informed decisions. Good brokers are continually looking for deals and are eager to work with active investors like you who want to buy properties. Brokers tend to specialize in one or two towns and don't have a monopoly on information, so I don't advise that you work exclusively with one. Let them compete for and earn your business. How do you find the best brokers? Find the brokers who generated the most sales and listings in your geographical target area and introduce yourself to them. Share your investment goals with them and request their assistance in finding properties that meet your specifications. Real estate brokers can be a tremendous source of valuable deal flow if you're working with the ones who have the information you need and are willing to pass it along to you.

Bankers, Mortgage Brokers, and Other Lenders

Bankers, mortgage brokers, and other lenders are astute at determining the optimal way to finance income-producing properties. They will provide you with the best options for obtaining mortgages. They will also assist you in determining the ideal way to reduce your current carrying costs by consolidating and/or refinancing your mortgages. Based on your particular circumstances (credit score, down payment amount, debt, employment status, income, and so on), they will determine which sorts of loans you are eligible for and the program that best meets your individual needs. At the end of the day, you want to work with someone who will be able to deliver the funds so that you can increase your property holdings. A good lender will review your situation and secure the least costly and most effective funding for your project.

Mentor

Everyone who wants to be a landlord or real estate investor should find himself at least one mentor. This is someone who already has all of the experience that you need. He has learned from the school of hard knocks and has unique knowledge that you might not be able to gain elsewhere. Your mentor may be retired or still be quite active in real estate investing. A good mentor will make time for you and guide you through the challenges of this business. Sure, you'll have a lawyer, accountant, mortgage broker, and real estate broker who can answer questions based on their particular expertise from time to time, but no one has the insight and full depth of empirical knowledge that your real estate mentor has. All of your team members will have very pronounced experience in their individual professions, but a mentor has experience in all of the areas that are critical to your business. Be sensitive to your mentor's time and never abuse your relationship by asking him for money for your own endeavors. Do not consume too much of your mentor's time with frivolous questions, and by all means do not forget that your mentor is probably the most irreplaceable asset on your team.

How do you find a mentor? Attend real estate investment clubs and sit next to the people with the gray hair. You also can call some of the larger real estate companies or property management firms in your area and request a meeting with the owner. If you develop a good relationship with one of these people, then you simply continue the dialogue. If this person responds to your questions and seems to enjoy being involved in your advancement, then you may have found yourself a mentor.

Colleagues and Fellow Investors

Unlike your mentor, your colleagues are people you can pester as often as necessary. Colleagues are people who have the same experience as you and perhaps are the same age. You and your colleagues are laboring in the trenches, trying to learn as much as possible while you avoid all of the pitfalls. If you have a new idea or a strategy that you are still developing, you can solicit feedback from colleagues. Certainly don't call your lawyer or your accountant to chitchat, because you'll be paying $150+ an hour for advice that you might be able to get for free from a colleague. Also, I don't recommend asking your real estate mentor, because he might be too busy, and you want to request his advice only when the idea is more fully developed. Your colleagues are your friends who are working as hard as you at developing real estate empires. Surround yourself with as many of these dedicated strivers as possible, and *always* try to give them as much as you take. Be helpful and share your knowledge and ideas with them—because it's indeed a wise truism that you get as much as you give.

Lessons Learned

- Your team members are a critical component of your success.
- Take your time and select your team carefully.
- Don't hesitate to let team members go if they aren't performing to your satisfaction.
- Find yourself a mentor and a few good colleagues who are willing to help you when you need advice and guidance.

15

Exit Strategy

Buy land, they've stopped making it.

— MARK TWAIN

An exit strategy in real estate investing is a plan for selling one or all of your properties so that you can retire, diversify your investment portfolio, return some capital to your bank account, or reinvest the proceeds to buy more real estate. Because you are probably a novice at real estate investing with many years until retirement, I recommend that you continue to reinvest all of your proceeds in real estate for many, many years to come.

You should be thinking about an exit strategy even before you close on a new property. In fact, the most successful investors I know have multiple exit strategies in place before they submit an offer letter. I'm certainly not advocating a quick sale for a marginal return, but I am suggesting that you determine when and how you are going to sell. Do you want to rent out the property for five years and sell if the price has increased by 25 or 50 percent? Do you want to buy and hold the property until you can convert the building to condos? Would an offer for your property at a 5 percent cap rate do it? Understand how and under what circumstances you're going to dispose of your portfolio. Understand how you are going to get out even before you get in.

Most real estate investors I know who have more than 30 years of experience wish that they'd never sold any of their properties. Some of them are disappointed when they look back at that magnificent five-family brick building they sold 25 years ago for $50,000—because it is now worth $1.5 million! I don't necessarily agree with the "buy and hold till you die" philosophy. If you can upgrade your properties from a class C (the lowest class) to an A or B and improve your returns, then it might make more sense to sell.

For instance, if you bought a property at a 10 percent cap rate and can sell it for a 4 percent cap rate and replace it with another property at a 12 percent cap rate using a 1031 tax exchange, then this certainly might be worth further investigation. If you can convert a property to condos and triple your money, then you should consider selling. If you want to liquidate your portfolio of smaller rental properties and buy a few larger buildings in a better location with improved cash flow and lower management expenses, then you should consider this opportunity. There are a multitude of tempting and viable alternatives for your investment dollars, and there's an opportunity cost for holding all of your capital in your existing portfolio. Consider all of your options and constantly evaluate the market for new opportunities that will maximize your return. Some of the primary indicators that alter the market in ways that allow you to sell a rental property for a premium without significantly altering the property or increasing its NOI are

1. *Low interest rates.* These provide an affordable way to acquire capital. Lower interest rates reduce the cost of carrying debt and make the financing of properties more affordable. Although rates eventually will increase, current interest rates have remained at or near their historical lows.
2. *Job growth.* New companies locate in the area or existing companies increase their hiring. This increases housing demand.

3. *Population growth.* Immigrants arrive from outside of the country or people migrate from other states. This increases housing demand in certain areas and reduces it in others.

4. *Low cap rate environment.* Cap rates change from time to time and are driven by several factors including interest rates, housing demand, the condition of the property, and market conditions. Average cap rates have historically hovered somewhere around 9 percent. If interest rates decline, housing demand can improve, condo conversions likely gain popularity, cap rates will decline, and the value of income-producing properties will increase.

5. *Changing neighborhoods.* Gentrification or the basic improvement of an area increases property values. For example, condo converters might target an entire street or neighborhood. They will make significant upgrades to buildings and improve the overall environment of an area in a very short time. Property owners (the individuals who buy these condos) tend to care for their homes and streets more than renters do, so prices will climb as the effects of gentrification take hold.

6. *Condo conversion opportunities.* Developers usually are willing to pay a premium based on the selling price of condos and not on the property's rental income, and this will increase the estimated value of apartment buildings. Condo conversion opportunities tend to be a function of points 1, 2, 3, and 5.

In addition to the six criteria just listed, successfully increasing the NOI on your property will enable you to sell it for a premium. Admittedly, you cannot alter interest rates, the overall demand for housing, population growth, or other macroeconomic factors that affect property values, but you most certainly can have a direct and powerful impact on the value of your properties by increasing their NOI. Before you sell, be sure to maximize your NOI so that a higher sales price is justifiable.

More units under one roof tend to provide better overall returns. However, you'll probably begin your career by buying a condo, a single-family home, or a one- to four-unit multifamily apartment building. That's how most small investors begin. After a few years, even if you aren't The Donald, you'll learn the inside secrets of the trade as you assume full responsibility for the management of your properties. In the worst-case scenario, your tenants will utterly exasperate you, and you'll quit, burn out, or, at the very least, reevaluate what you're doing. You'll have received one too many midnight calls from irate tenants demanding that you visit the property and deal with their clogged toilets. As you consider all of your options, an ideal alternative to throwing in the towel is to consolidate your portfolio of bothersome smaller properties and exchange them for a larger building, where you can hire a property management company to deal with the day-to-day headaches. I reached that point myself after my third year in the business. If you have a higher threshold for aggravation and annoyance than I did, perhaps you'll be able to manage all of your properties until retirement. But I recommend concentrating your time and energy on growing your business and leaving the mundane, day-to-day tasks to others.

That said, you must sell or extract equity from your current portfolio in order to consolidate and buy larger buildings. If you decide to sell, consider selling your least-profitable properties in the worst locations. If you have a class C property in a class C area with a return that simply does not compare with the return on your other assets, then this is the ideal holding to jettison first. Try to remove any emotion from the decision-making process and let your financial spreadsheet make the final decision. Compare all of your rental properties over the past 12 to 24 months to formulate the optimal liquidation strategy. Top-performing properties with the greatest potential for future appreciation should stay, and poor performers should go. Finally, you should try postponing a sale until you have something else in the pipeline to buy. The generous tax benefits of exchanging one investment property for another are worth considering.

1031 Tax Exchanges

If you decide to sell one of your income-producing properties and reinvest the funds in another one, you may use the proceeds from the sale to buy another property and defer all taxes on the gain from the sale if you use a 1031 tax exchange. If you do sell an income-producing property and plan to buy another one, you should definitely use the 1031 method to delay the payment of taxes. The property you sell is called the *relinquished property*, and the new property is called the *replacement property*. The laws that govern the 1031 tax exchange are very strict, so you must know all of the rules in order to defer the taxes on the transaction.

Before closing the sale on the relinquished property, you'll need to know a qualified intermediary who specializes in 1031 tax exchanges (your lawyer will likely be able to refer you to several companies). The licensed intermediary must take the requisite precautions to preserve the tax-deferred transaction. Any proceeds from the sale are given directly to the intermediary after the sale. You won't receive any funds at the closing, but you'll be able to verify the amount being sent to the intermediary by examining the "summary of seller's transaction" column of your settlement statement. You then have 45 days to identify one or more properties of "like kind" and 180 days to close on your transaction(s). The 180-day period is not counted from the date you identify the property or from the 45-day mark; rather, the 180-day limit commences on the day you sell the relinquished property. If you can do these things within the specified times, the net proceeds from your sale can be used to acquire the new property, and you do not have to pay capital gains tax on the original sale (at least for the time being, because the tax obligation is only deferred, not forgiven).

What is a property of like kind, anyway? According to the requirements of Section 1031, property held "for productive use in a trade or business" or "for investment purposes" is acceptable. Like-kind property is any other form of investment property—essentially other real estate, regardless of whether it's the same kind of property. The replacement property could be a multifamily apartment building, condominium, single-family home, plot of land, warehouse, strip mall, or office building. The replacement property cannot, however, be real estate for your personal use, which would not meet the 1031 guidelines.

If you don't use the 1031 tax exchange or don't comply with the time requirements just outlined, you'll need to pay the capital gains tax, which at the time of this writing is 15 percent (long-term capital gains). This rate is actually quite favorable, considering it's the lowest it's been in history (see the table that follows). Some investors actually prefer paying their capital gains taxes now, because they are certain that the rate will climb substantially in the future. Their argument is logical, because they at least know how much they owe today and are willing to pay it now, instead of risking the possibility of paying substantially more in the future. In addition to the federal tax rate of 15 percent, you also may have to pay state taxes, depending on where you live. For additional information, visit the IRS Web site at www.irs.gov or consult a tax accountant.

Capital Gains Tax

Term	Holding Period	Maximum Tax Rate
Short term	Less than or equal to one year	38.6%
Long term	More than one year	15%

Perhaps an example of a 1031 exchange would help to better explain this concept.

Let's consider the following scenario: in 1999 you acquired a multi-family rental property for $300,000, and on August 5, 2006, it's worth $500,000. Leaving aside expenses, depreciation, and capital improvements, which are typically used in calculating the actual profit from the transaction, your gain from this sale would be $200,000. Because the capital gains tax rate is 15 percent, you'd be required to pay the Internal Revenue Service $30,000. The taxes you save by using the exchange can then be used to buy a bigger and better property. In this example, you'll have another $30,000 of purchasing power if you use the 1031 tax exchange. All of the proceeds ($200,000) from the relinquished property must be used to buy the new real estate. You are not able to use any of the profit from the sale for any purpose other than to buy the replacement property.

As mentioned, if you sell a property using a 1031 tax exchange, all of the net sales proceeds will be held by the intermediary. Within 45 days from the day the property is sold, you must identify the replacement property or properties and advise the qualified intermediary of your choices, in writing. The intermediary will request that you submit a list of the property addresses. For example:

1. 1212 Main Street, New York, NY
2. 1515 South Street, Miami, FL
3. 2020 West Street, Los Angeles, CA

Because there must be a purchase within 180 days after the relinquished property was sold, you'll have until February 5, 2007, to close on one or more of the properties identified. At the closing for the replacement property, the intermediary will send your lawyer a check for the amount in the escrow account (less the intermediary's fee). These funds will reduce or eliminate the amount you owe at the closing. Once again, ask your lawyer for a copy of the settlement statement before closing so that you can review all of the numbers and make corrections, should there be any errors.

Primary Residence

Tax benefits aren't confined solely to income-producing properties. They also apply to your primary residence, and these are, in my opinion, incredibly valuable tax benefits that you should utilize. These benefits, started by the IRS in 1997, offer an unparalleled method for increasing your net worth while avoiding capital gains. Unlike the 1031 tax exchange, where you are only deferring capital gains taxes until a future date, the primary residence tax laws don't require you to pay them at all.

The rules work like this: if you have lived in your home for two of the past five years, the first $250,000 of any profit is tax-exempt if you're single, and the first $500,000 is exempt if you're married. Any profits in excess of those amounts are taxed at the capital gains rate (15 percent). If the reason for the sale is a change in employment, a relocation out of the state, an illness of a family member, or an unforeseen circumstance such as divorce, then a partial exemption is even possible. Furthermore, there's no limit to how often you can do this (so long as you live in the home for two of the five years before selling). If you're smart, you'll use the profits from the sale of your primary residence to buy income-producing properties. The more assets you acquire, the better. This is truly one of the best opportunities you will ever find. Can you think of another way you can earn $500,000 and pay absolutely *no* taxes? You can think long and hard, but it's unlikely that you'll be able to think of anything even remotely comparable.

Increasing Your Net Worth

Without a doubt, in the past decade, home ownership has been the most effective tool for increasing net worth. And, building wealth through home ownership is relatively easy compared to most other methods. After buying a home with a reasonable amount of leverage (typically using a 3 to 20 percent down payment), you wait and allow appreciation and inflation to work their remarkable magic. The appreciation (6 percent annually since 1975) might not seem that stellar when compared with other investments, but an annual increase of more than 10 percent has been commonplace during the past five years in most coastal towns. Let's assume that you acquired a property for $500,000 with a 10 percent down payment, or $50,000. If it appreciates by 10 percent in the first year of ownership, the property will be worth $550,000. That's a $50,000 gain, or a 100 percent return on your initial investment of $50,000. Where else can you obtain such amazing returns? This is precisely why so many people love real estate.

Buy and Flip or Buy and Rent

If your strategy is to buy, renovate, and sell, then you must be careful and have multiple exit strategies. If interest rates rise, then it will be more difficult for you to sell your property, and your carrying costs might increase. However, if you always buy only properties where the numbers still make sense even if you must rent the units, you'll always have a Plan B. Instead of selling, you can always rent the units and wait to sell until market conditions are more favorable.

Lessons Learned

- Determine how you're going to get out before you get in. Always have multiple exit strategies even before you buy a property.
- Constantly reevaluate the market for unique opportunities to sell off a property and maximize your return.

Exit Strategy

- Sell or refinance your portfolio so that you can upgrade your properties to larger apartment buildings in better areas.
- Use 1031 tax exchanges; they are an ideal way to defer taxes on property dispositions.
- You must identify replacement property within 45 days if using a 1031 tax exchange.
- You must close on one or more of the identified properties within 180 days.
- Use a qualified intermediary who will complete that part of the transaction. Ask your attorney for referrals.
- The tax rate on long-term capital gains is 15 percent should you sell a property without using a 1031 tax exchange.

16

How to Succeed in Today's Competitive Market

Every day I get up and look through the Forbes list
of the richest people in America. If I'm not there, I
go to work.

—ROBERT ORBEN

When I started investing in real estate, I was buying properties at extremely favorable cap rates, and each one of them generated a positive cash flow within 90 days—even with 100 percent leverage. Admittedly, the landscape today has changed dramatically, in part because of the astounding appreciation realized over the past five years and in part because of the condo craze, which continues to defy gravity. Real estate has taken center stage and become the investment of choice ever since alternative investment choices such as stocks and bonds began providing diminishing returns. The Internet bubble implosion in 2000, coupled with the terrorist attacks in 2001 and the Enron fiasco, cast an ominous cloud over the stock market. Today, investors lack confidence in Wall Street, do not trust the executives who run corporate America, and fear that another terrorist attack could undermine the markets once again. They've been expressing their dissatisfaction by pulling their money out of the equity markets and reallocating their investment dollars to a tangible investment like real estate—an investment that provides more control, and one that is insulated from the negative influences of corporate scandals and improper accounting practices.

Today, there are more individuals investing in real estate than ever before. Some are veterans with decades of experience in both good and bad markets, but many are novice investors and speculators trying to make a quick buck. The day traders of the late 1990s have made the transition into the real estate market and are now buying and flipping properties instead of stocks. They may not really know or fully understand what they're doing, but they continue to make money—and continue to make it difficult for individuals who are serious about long-term real estate investing. Given the market conditions, both veteran investors and speculators are buying rundown properties, renovating them, and quickly selling them off to the highest bidder. Here's an example of a recent listing in the *Miami Herald*:

> *6 bed, 6 bath, 5,800 sq ft–Asking price: $839,000*
> *The property's sales history was as follows:*
>   *June 1992 sold for: $11,000*
>   *October 1995 sold for: $135,000*
>   *September 2003 sold for: $225,000*
>   *October 2003 sold for: $365,000*
>   *October 2005 asking price: $839,000*

In 13 years, the price (if the property sells at the asking price) will have increased by $828,000! Is that possible? When you're evaluating a property, you must look up the property's sales history to see when the current owner purchased it, and for how much. Do you really think this property could have appreciated by $474,000 ($839,000 minus $365,000) in two years, considering that only minor and inexpensive upgrades had been made since October 2003? Investors and speculators are also acquiring apartment buildings and converting them to condominiums for massive profits. As long as the demand for condos remains strong and the price of alternative housing remains out of reach for the average household, the condo play will be the only game in town. Moreover, REITs and pension funds continue to plow money into the real estate sector, and this has created a ripple-down effect for everyone in the food chain. The economics of many rental properties in some markets no longer make sense, and this may cause you a great deal of frustration as you search to find a property that is cash flow positive with a reasonable down payment.

We are currently in a condo-driven market that is punctuated by extremely low interest rates and an ample supply of buyers (see Figure 16.1). Rental buildings are being sold at cap rates that were once considered unthinkable. Condo converters are acquiring apartment buildings based on the conversion economics and not rental revenue. In some of the country's hottest condo markets (Manhattan, Miami, Los Angeles,

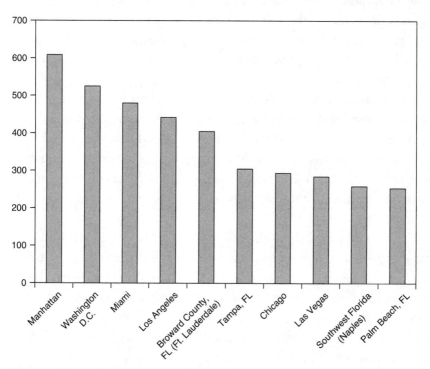

Figure 16.1 Apartment-to-Condo Conversion Deals: Sales Volume (in Millions)

SOURCE: *Real Capital Analytics Multifamily Executive* magazine, August 2005, p. 50.

Washington, D.C., Chicago, and Las Vegas), multifamily buildings would fail to produce a positive cash flow even with a down payment of more than 50 percent and an interest-only mortgage.

Only 1.8 percent of all apartment buildings acquired in 2001 were purchased by condo converters. By 2004, 14.6 percent of all apartment buildings acquired were purchased by condo converters. If the trend continues along this trajectory, cap rates will continue to fall, making it increasingly difficult to acquire an apartment building for rental purposes and generate a positive cash flow. The situation has become even more challenging because rents have not kept pace with the appreciating values and have either stabilized or decreased.

If you buy a multifamily apartment building at an unreasonable premium, you'd better be prepared to deal with negative cash flow—and I would certainly not recommend buying a property with negative cash flow. That said, these conditions are ripe for selling and reinvesting the proceeds in less competitive markets (where you can acquire properties at higher cap rates). Some of the largest property owners (see Figure 16.2) are selling off apartment buildings and repositioning their portfolios for the decade ahead.

These apartment owners fully comprehend that the compressed cap rate environment has given them a unique opportunity to convert their apartment stock to condos or to sell the worst-performing properties for a premium. If the big guys are doing it, then the smaller-sized investors will follow suit. Don't get caught paying condo conversion prices if you have an apartment rental strategy. You simply won't survive this fatal mistake.

The condo conversion value play has proved to be quite lucrative for most players, but no one can accurately predict when the good times will come to an end. You certainly don't want to be the last person holding an overpriced property that is losing money each month because it can't sustain itself as a rental property and can't be sold off as individual condos because the demand has suddenly dried up. Many speculators will go broke when they find themselves in this position, and prices for apartment buildings will eventually return to reasonable levels, which will be the ideal time to buy.

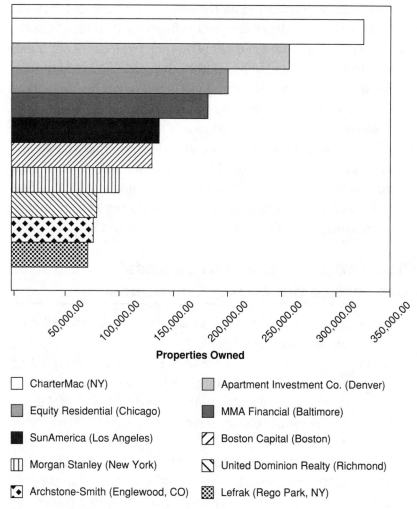

Figure 16.2 Top 10 Apartment Owners
SOURCE: NREI magazine, July 2005, p. 36, www.nreionline.com.

So, what must you do to succeed in the meantime? Look in areas and neighborhoods where condo conversion is not yet feasible so that sellers are not demanding or expecting that a condo premium be paid for their properties. Consider alternative strategies like development or condo conversions until either the market changes or you find a deal that makes sense. Just be careful not to be caught when the market changes. Buy a mixed-use property (residential and commercial units), sell off the residential units as condos, pay off the entire mortgage, and keep the commercial units (typically on the ground floor) for their cash flow. Or, buy two separate apartment buildings in one purchase, condo one building, pay down the mortgage, and keep the other building as a long-term rental if it will generate positive cash flow. Continue to think out of the box, just as long as you are making money and enjoying what you're doing. Take your time to find properties that make good financial sense and don't lose your patience or force a deal to work. Once you do find the ideal rental property, move quickly to add it to your portfolio. Great deals exist in every town and during every type of market condition (hot or cold). Be patient yet persistent in your search, run your numbers, perform a thorough due diligence, and close on the winners.

Follow These "16 Steps to Success" Regardless of the Market Conditions

1. Find an experienced mentor and group of colleagues who will help you achieve your real estate goals.
2. Extend your network as far as possible. Don't be shy about letting people know that you're searching for income-producing properties. Locate profitable deals by using LoopNet, the MLS, real estate brokers, your personal network, direct mailings, contacts with other property owners, and so on.
3. If you don't hire a property management company, you'll need to live close enough to your properties to manage them. Being an absentee landlord, especially in the beginning of your landlord career, can prove disastrous. I had a 30-minute drive rule when I began, so I didn't buy properties more than 30 minutes from my own home. If you decide to hire a management company, remember to negotiate the fee and link the company's pay to its performance.
4. Check and verify numbers. Don't accept the information on operating expenses and rental income provided to you by the broker or property owner as being accurate.
5. Make sure you can address renters' complaints, and have reliable vendors (plumbers, carpenters, and electricians) to help you with property repairs.

6. Secure financing. Obtain funds from banks, private lenders, investment partners, home equity loans, or hard-money lenders. Try to secure the down payment funds in advance of any purchase.

7. Present offers that make good financial sense. Buy with immediate equity. Buy only properties that provide you with an equity position from day one. You must find properties that generate a positive cash flow.

8. Close on the property. Easier said than done, right? There are a thousand factors that can derail a closing. If it's a good deal that you simply can't pass up, then don't let that happen. Close on the property as soon as possible and begin to implement your NOI increasing strategy. Don't argue about 1/2 percent on the interest rate or minor punch-list items. Concentrate on the big picture and close the deal.

9. Have a strategy of increasing NOI. Improve the value of the property by raising the NOI (net operating income). Increase revenue and decrease operating expenses.

10. Screen your renters thoroughly. Your first impression might be positive, but if you dig further into a person's past, you may have cause to think otherwise.

11. Maintain detailed files and contracts on all of your tenants. Manage your rental properties as a business.

12. Set aside sufficient reserves to cover vacancies, renovations, and deferred maintenance that you may not have anticipated. Have enough cash reserves on hand to weather a downturn in the market. Sell the property for a substantial profit and buy bigger properties with higher returns that are situated in better locations. The bigger the building, the better the return. Capitalize on the economies of scale that a larger building offers. Consolidate property management and maintenance to reduce expenses.

13. Know your exit strategy. In fact, establish multiple exit strategies so that you can dispose of your property at some point in the future. Manage tax implications after the sale. Use 1031 tax exchanges and hold properties for a minimum of one year to reduce tax obligations.

14. Think unconventionally. If you can't find an income-producing property that makes good financial sense, then start looking elsewhere. Perhaps there are more opportunities farther away from your target

market. Would you consider buying a property out of your state and hiring a property manager to deal with the day-to-day activities? Perhaps you might consider buying a condo, a single-family home, or some other property that you can renovate and sell for a profit. You could use the proceeds from the sale to buy an even larger multi-family property. Don't be a speculator, but if a stellar deal comes your way, a renovation project might prove to be a profitable endeavor while you look for a moneymaking rental building. Maybe you just need more time to deepen your network of real estate brokers, lawyers, and property owners to locate the right property. Whatever you do, don't give up! Remember, 95 percent of would-be investors quit before they find the right property because they think it's too hard or they manage to convince themselves that the market is too competitive. The deals exist, but they won't be handed to you on a silver platter. You have to dedicate all of your energy to finding them.

15. Extract the equity from your properties or sell them to buy more properties. Use OPM (other people's money) to buy properties. Try to make the smallest possible down payment while maintaining a reasonable level of cash flow and debt-to-service ratios.

16. Stay with your day job until your properties can sustain your standard of living. Don't forget the cost of health insurance once you leave your day job. And, most important, have some fun and be passionate about your work.

Characteristics of Successful Real Estate Investors

Most successful real estate investors have a burning desire to be in charge of their own destiny. Successful investors are motivated to do what most other people are incapable of doing. Everyone needs a reason to get up in the morning and dedicate his time, enthusiasm, and energy to a particular cause. Successful investors might be motivated by the challenge, by the financial reward, or by the opportunity to be their own boss. Whatever their reason, a catalyst of change exists for them, and it's a powerful one.

Entrepreneurial Ability

Some individuals are wonderful employees and highly capable at what they do. They make a very good salary and grow accustomed to that lifestyle. They may fly first class, have access to a substantial business expense account, and be well respected in their industry. They avoid being their own boss because they view entrepreneurship as a risky endeavor. Entrepreneurs don't fear being their own boss; in fact, they embrace the opportunity to assume full responsibility for their future. Natural-born entrepreneurs understand the inherent risks of owning their own business and manage the risks accordingly. Entrepreneurs enjoy the independence, challenge, and financial reward of starting their own business. They also understand that during the first few years, they may fail to produce the income they were generating at their day job; however, over the course of time, their earnings will eventually dwarf anything they could possibly generate by working for someone else. The richest people in the world, the late Sam Walton of Wal-Mart and Bill Gates of Microsoft, are entrepreneurs who would never have obtained such great financial riches had they worked for someone else.

Industry Knowledge

You can learn about real estate by reading books like this one, you can take classes offered at local universities and colleges, or you can go to work for a real estate company. However you do it, you should learn as much as possible, gain empirical experience, and then set off on your own. Knowledge is a critical part of your foundation for success. I suggest attending a real estate agent preparation class and obtaining your real estate salesperson's license. You may not be interested in selling real estate, but the knowledge is worthwhile. When buying and selling your properties, you might even be eligible for a commission. Also, take the general contractor's class and examination in your state. You'll eventually need to renovate an apartment, or you'll begin a development project (renovation of an existing property or a new construction project). Even if you don't want to obtain permits because of the liability issues, you will understand state building codes better, and this knowledge will help you to manage contractors. I would also recommend obtaining your property management certification. After earning this certification, you'll know more about managing multifamily apartment buildings, your legal rights as a property owner or manager, and financial analysis and accounting practices for your real estate business.

Decisive Nature and Ability to Make Decisions

You need to be able to make decisions based on thorough research and intuition. You often need to evaluate opportunities very quickly and act on them immediately. Have you ever heard the phrase *paralysis by analysis*? You mustn't overanalyze deals because you'll waste too much time thinking and you'll find too many reasons to justify not moving forward. The answer is to act more and analyze a reasonable amount, so that you avoid paralysis by analysis. There's a fine balance between making a decision based on thorough research into all the facts and figures and simply knowing what a good deal is and seizing the opportunity. With more experience, you'll be able to tell the great deals from the average ones, but until then, you'll need to take managed risks and get started.

Ability to Execute a Plan

Some people are wonderful planners and talk a good game. They can create a stunning 100-page business plan, but they don't have the ability to execute the plan they've written. To be a successful real estate investor, you need to create a solid plan and make it a reality. You cannot take no as an answer and you must never quit. Find a way to move mountains when most others say it can't be done.

Real estate has always been a good investment, and it continues to be a fairly stable place for individuals to invest. Real estate investors have accumulated some of the greatest fortunes in history. However, success as an investor ultimately depends on your work ethic and your ability to manage risk.

These days, working hard just isn't enough to guarantee financial success. How many people do you know who work hard? How many of those individuals are truly wealthy? Very few, right? There's no proven or direct correlation between working hard and being affluent. One needs to work both hard and smart to succeed.

Cash Flow

Cash flow is king! Without cash flow, you'll go broke very quickly. If you have substantial positive cash flow, then you'll be able to finance new deals and can manage your business with greater ease. Property owners should have little patience with late payments from their tenants. Late payments will have a direct and negative impact on your cash flow. I tend to be very lenient with good tenants who just happen to be going through a difficult financial time, but I can also be tough when I feel that a tenant is taking advantage of the situation. Evicting a tenant is not an easy process, and it is riddled with very specific laws. Understanding the eviction process (refer to Chapter 11, "Basic Tenant–Landlord Law") and filing for an eviction quickly can save you costly delays and months of lost rent. Filing a Notice to Quit (see Appendix D for a sample form) is the first step in the process and typically gets a late-paying tenant's attention.

Try to set aside money for maintenance, capital expenditures, and vacancies. This will prevent temporary cash flow problems from sinking the ship. You'll eventually need to replace a hot water tank, improve landscaping, paint an apartment, or caulk a tub. Save enough money from the rent to pay for these repairs. Obviously, the goal is to keep good tenants in your properties at all times. Vacancies are costly and will reduce your cash flow. Limit the vacancy period by finding a qualified tenant as quickly as possible and keeping your tenants content. I try to save $200 to $300 per unit per year for all capital expenditures (i.e., major renovations). Capital expenditures are major improvements. They are generally depreciated over their useful life (let your accountant determine these numbers), and are different from operational repairs, which are subtracted from a property's income during the year in which the expense was incurred.

Lessons Learned

- The competition for apartment buildings is fierce.
- Condo converters, speculators, REITs, and pension funds are investing heavily in the real estate sector and continue to push prices to greater heights.

- Don't compete with condo converters. They can make money in the conversion process, but you'll lose your shirt if you pay a condo conversion price and maintain the property as a rental.
- Take your time in finding profitable deals. Be patient, and don't force a property to work if the numbers don't make sense.
- Don't give up! Good deals exist in every market, but you need to be persistent and relentless to find them.

17

Leaving Your Day Job

*Change is the law of life, and those who look only to
the past and present are certain to miss the future.*

—JOHN F. KENNEDY

I have started each new chapter with a quote. I hope you have found
them both motivational and inspiring. To end this book, I will leave
you with my favorite quote of all, one that I display on the wall in my
office, where I can read it each and every day:

> Every morning in Africa a gazelle wakes up. It knows it must run faster than the
> fastest lion or it will be killed. Every morning a lion wakes up. It knows it must
> outrun the slowest gazelle or it will starve to death. It doesn't matter whether you
> are a lion or a gazelle—when the sun comes up, you had better be running.
>
> —UNKNOWN

Rise from bed each morning and run as fast as you can toward your
dreams. Don't slow down, and certainly never give up. You'll have good

days and bad days, but you must remember to always keep moving forward. For every 100 individuals who don't believe in your ability to achieve your dreams, there will be one person who encourages you to continue at all costs. Listen to that one voice, even if it happens to be your own. There's a never-ending supply of pundits and nonbelievers in this world who will find countless reasons to justify why something can't be done; these people seldom take many risks and rarely obtain financial independence. Don't make the same mistake.

Just what is financial independence? Well, it's the freedom that wealth can bring to your life; it releases you from the day-to-day problems of self-preservation and survival that the vast majority of the world experiences on a daily basis. Wealth enables you to live without the fear of a catastrophic financial loss. Financial independence also provides you with more control over your life. You can go where and when you want and still meet your financial obligations. Finally, wealth enables you to be more altruistic with your resources and to support causes you believe in. Your wealth can also be given to others who need your help. When you obtain financial independence, you'll be able to help yourself, your family, and others who truly need your generosity to fulfill their own dreams.

After you've accumulated enough rental properties to provide you with a cash flow that meets or exceeds your current salary, you'll be in a position to consider leaving your day job. You are the only person who can ultimately determine when to leave. After all, you may have grown accustomed to the corporate womb and its perceived trappings of security. You might not want to venture out into the "real world," where you'll have to fend completely for yourself. I'm confident, however, that after reading this book, you'll embrace the opportunity to leave your day job and embark on a new and exciting business of your own. It is my sincere hope that when the right time comes, you'll make that leap of faith and say good-bye to the 9-to-5 world. In its place, you'll opt for 100 percent control of your destiny, greater financial compensation for your efforts, more rewarding work, and the ability to help others after you've made it. It's a decision you won't regret.

Good luck with your investing, and by all means please let me know how you are progressing.

Feel free to e-mail me at: matt@landlordandinvestor.com.

Appendix A
MORE QUOTES

I don't believe in circumstances. The people who get on in this world are the people who get up and look for the circumstances they want, and, if they can't find them, make them.

—GEORGE BERNARD SHAW

—▪ ▪—

It is not the strongest of species that survive, nor the most intelligent, but the one most responsive to change.

—CHARLES DARWIN

—▪ ▪—

Skate to where the puck is going to be, not where it's been.

—WAYNE GRETZKY

—▪ ▪—

Go confidently in the direction of your dreams! Live the life you've imagined.

—HENRY DAVID THOREAU

Appendix A

A pessimist sees the difficulty in every opportunity; an optimist sees the opportunity in every difficulty.

—Sir Winston Churchill

Anything in life worth having is worth working for.

—Andrew Carnegie

Half of being smart is knowing what you're dumb at.

—Solomon Short

Happiness is nothing more than good health and a poor memory.

—Albert Schweitzer

Every time history repeats itself, the price goes up.

—Unknown

Anyone who has never made a mistake has never tried anything new.

—Albert Einstein

Carpe diem. Seize the day, boys. Make your lives extraordinary.

—Robin Williams (from the movie Dead Poets Society)

Do not follow where the path may lead. Go instead where there is no path and leave a trail.

—George Bernard Shaw

Energy and persistence conquer all things.

—Benjamin Franklin

More Quotes

Far and away the best prize that life offers is the chance to work hard at something worth doing.

—THOMAS JEFFERSON

The key to success is for you to make a habit throughout your life of doing the things you fear.

—VINCENT VAN GOGH

Genius is 1% inspiration and 99% perspiration.

—THOMAS EDISON

When one door closes another door opens; but we so often look so long and so regretfully upon the closed door, that we do not see the ones which open for us.

—ALEXANDER GRAHAM BELL

Life all comes down to a few moments. This is one of them.

—BUD FOX, STOCKBROKER (FROM THE MOVIE *WALL STREET*)

I'd like to live as a poor man with lots of money.

—PABLO PICASSO

Waste your money and you're only out of money, but waste your time and you've lost a part of your life.

—MICHAEL LEBOEUF

Singleness of purpose is one of the chief essentials for success in life.

—JOHN D. ROCKEFELLER JR.

Appendix A

— —

If you get up one more time than you fall, you will make it through.

—CHINESE PROVERB

It frees you from doing things you dislike. Since I dislike doing nearly everything, money is handy.

—GROUCHO MARX

— —

Money will buy you a pretty good dog, but it won't buy the wag of his tail.

HENRY WHEELER SHAW

— —

A rich man is nothing but a poor man with money.

—W. C. FIELDS

— —

It's good to have money and the things that money can buy, but it's good, too, to check up once in a while and make sure that you haven't lost the things that money can't buy.

—GEORGE HORACE LORIMER

Appendix B

TYCOON
IN THE MAKING

Boston real estate investor, Matthew Martinez, traded a high-tech career for a gig as landlord.

June 17, 2004: 10:10 AM EDT

By Sarah Max, CNN/Money senior writer

BEND, Ore. (CNN/Money)–Matthew Martinez was working as the director of international business development at Internet company Terra Lycos in 2001 when he got a business idea of his own—pool investors' money and buy apartment buildings in the Boston area.

"I created an 82-page business plan for what I wanted to do and pitched it to everyone I knew with money," said Matt, now 34. "I couldn't find anyone to invest."

So on a much smaller scale, he decided to go it alone, setting his sights on three-family buildings in Dorchester, a Boston neighborhood.

About that time, as luck would have it, Matt befriended a seasoned real estate investor who was buying a unit in the building where Matt lived.

"We hit it off, and he took me under his wing" said Matt.

Three years later Matt has $1.3 million worth of equity in five multifamily buildings in Dorchester and one single-family rehab in the well-to-do Boston suburb Wellesley.

Better yet, his rental income yields enough cash that Matt quit his day job in April to be a full-time landlord.

Here's how he turned an 82-page idea into a career. (To read the full story go to http://money.cnn.com/2004/06/16/real_estate/investment_prop/tycoon_martinez/index.htm.)

Response to CNN/Money Article: A Few E-mails from Inspired Investors; Articles, and So On

Matt,

Thank you for calling me back earlier today. The article about you was great and inspired me to step up my efforts in real estate investment.

As I mentioned, I'm trying to put together a similar plan of investment here in Arizona and would really appreciate it, if possible, for you to mail me your real estate business plan. If I can ever help you with any Arizona real estate info, please let me know.

Thank you,

Phoenix, AZ

Matt,

I have had some great interest in doing exactly what you have done, but I just haven't taken that first step. I might be coming into a little bit of money soon and I am ready to take that first step. Would you ever be interested in mentoring somebody? Would love to sit down and talk to you sometime. Look forward to hearing from you.

Columbus, OH

Matt:

Thanks for meeting with me yesterday. . . . It is great to hear what can be accomplished. I am dying to get that first one under my belt. As with other things in life, getting that first one under your belt is a big thing . . .

Tycoon in the Making

Extending the metaphor, I know I am going to have to put in a lot of time and effort to bag that first one, too. Can you send me that spreadsheet you talked about? Have a Happy Thanksgiving.

Seattle, WA

Matthew— I have much to learn . . . I would ideally like to get out of corporate America in the next 5 years so I can do real estate development/investing.

Miami, Florida

Matthew—

My two partners (a Real Estate Agent/Business Owner, and a Loan Officer/Business Owner) and I are in the process of creating a Real Estate Investment LLC. We are currently in contract on a 600 square foot luxury condo ($415,000) on the 12th floor at the Residence at the MGM Grand (Strip View) and a two bedroom Penthouse Condo, two blocks off the Strip ($359,000). Would you be interested in investing?

Las Vegas, NV

Matthew—

I am a new investor stuck on implementing the right strategy. Would you be able to meet and give me some advice?

I live in Brookline and can meet at your convenience. I need to hear a broader perspective.

Please let me know.

Brookline, MA

Matthew—I have been working to make my first investment property in Dartmouth break-even. I am close. Now I want to generate some cash flow with more properties but haven't chosen a strategy. My credit is good but I am heavily leveraged. I would be interested to learn more about what you are doing and how you chose to proceed. Could we meet in a week or so?

Dartmouth, NH

—▶ ◀—

Hey Matthew,

I just read about you and decided to look you up via craigslist. Two years ago I bought my first duplex here in Ann Arbor, MI. I'm doing well but I want to expand and eventually leave my job. Would it be possible for you to be a mentor to me. I'm 33— a psychologist with a good steady job but I want to be free from "the man" before I'm 40!

So if you would be willing to help me out I'd greatly appreciate it. Let me know what you think.

Ann Arbor, MI

—▶ ◀—

Hi Matt,

I had seen the CNN.com Millionaire in the Making piece on you some time ago and then coincidentally my sister ended up meeting you. It's a very impressive article. Congratulations on your success in your new career. I'm in the IT industry, like you were. It's a good living and I studied computer science many years ago for this type of job, but I've just found myself, as of lately (3-4 years), very much interested in property investing. I haven't quit my day job yet, but I really think I'd like to!

Hawaii, like San Diego and other areas, has just gone crazy. I'm just starting off, mostly to try to upgrade my own level of living, but I have begun to do some small investing. Rents have skyrocketed as well with some places well supported by the military. I have a small apt. that with each renter moving out I've been able to raise the rent. The military base housing allowance supports these increases as well. One area I've invested in is the resort home market. There are several resort home areas in Hawaii; on Oahu and the outer islands. The market, still surprisingly, looks like it supports flipping, but even seems to have enough legs to warrant holding on to the property for a short while for larger gains. Do you have any thoughts on the resort home market? Most of the talk I hear is about how the baby boomers will continue to feed this market for the next few years.

Tycoon in the Making

If all goes well, I should be in a position to continue investing. The property I'm moving into will be completed shortly and has gained quite a bit of equity already. I'm really interested in the next step. I haven't enough ideas yet. Should I continue with acquiring properties or try to take a larger step; perhaps something like a small 6-10? unit walkup apt building? I've looked into this a little—but, as all real estate now, it seems to be getting out of reach . . . maybe? I'd welcome any ideas or opportunities you have. Perhaps we can share ideas on our perspective areas 6,000 miles away!

Aloha!

Hawaii

——— ———

Matthew:

I'm still working my rear end off . . . still one of the ants. . . . I spent the weekend going over all of my monthly expenses to figure out what I needed to make monthly so my wife can quit her job and be home when my son gets off the bus from school. I have come to the conclusion that there are not enough hours in the day to do everything I need to do.

Chicago, IL

——— ———

Dear Matthew,

I saw the cnnfn.com article on you. Based on what's in the article, I extend a hearty "Congratulations" on doing so well!

I am writing to you because I seem to be interested in some of the same things you are. I am a 33-year-old landlord on two properties in Boston. I'd love to find out more about the Boston Landlord Association and whether I may participate! I am a practicing attorney in Boston with my real estate broker license, interested in doing a lot more with real estate.

Please let me know if you'd be up for meeting/talking to exchange real estate thoughts and expanding each of our respective networks.

Thank you,

Boston, MA

——— ———

Appendix B

Hi Matthew,

I just got off the phone with you. I am 32 years old and a landlord in San Diego. I own two 3-family properties within a few blocks of each other. I'd love to be on your mailing list and participate in your monthly meetings. The CNN article about you describes where I'd like to be in 5 years!

In case you're interested, some of the topics that interest me as a new real-estate investor are:

creating a company to own the property to limit my liability

best mortgaging strategies to maximize my ability to buy more property

partnering with other investors to buy larger properties

Thanks!

San Diego, CA

—▸ ◂—

Matthew–

I saw your article—it's very impressive what you've been able to do with your real estate.

I am trying to do somewhat of the same thing and would love to be in your position a few years from now. I live in Brighton, MA, and bought my first property in 2002, my second in 2003 and am looking for another place this year, but I don't think I'm making much progress and don't see my investments taking off much.

I'm sure you're very busy, but it would be great to meet up and pick your brain for a while—I'm not sure if this is something you'd be interested in, but if so, I'd like to talk.

Boston, MA

—▸ ◂—

I recently read an article on Matthew Martinez in Boston and I too am a young female that is doing a similar thing as he. I would like to make contact with him and am hoping that you could forward my information to him, if possible. I have multiple real estate properties in Washington, D.C. and Annapolis, MD etc.

Washington, D.C.

—▸ ◂—

Sarah,

Would it be possible to get some contact info for Matt Martinez? I used to work with him and would greatly appreciate it if I could get in contact with him about investing in real estate, because I, too, want to leave my day job.
Thanks,

Boston, MA

— ▶ ◀ —

Matt—I am sitting here in a cube watching everyone walk by South Station thinking there has got to be a better way. . . .

Boston, MA

Appendix C

SUGGESTED READING

Are You Missing the Real Estate Boom?, by David Lereah

Buying and Managing Residential Real Estate, by Andrew James McLean

The Complete Guide to Buying and Selling Apartment Buildings, by Steve Berges

Getting Started in Real Estate Investing, by Michael Thomsett

Home Improvement 1-2-3, by Home Depot

How to Build a Real Estate Empire, by Marcel Arsenault, John Hamilton, Ben Leeds, and Gerald Marcil

Inspecting a House, by Rex Cauldwell

Landlording, by Leigh Robinson

Landlording and Property Management, by Mark Weiss and Dan Baldwin

Maverick Real Estate Investing, by Steve Bergsman

The Millionaire Next Door, by Dr. Tom Stanley and Dr. Bill Danko

Appendix C

The Millionaire Real Estate Investor, by Gary Keller

Real Estate Dealmaking, by George Donohue

The Real Estate Millionaire: How to Invest in Rental Markets and Make a Fortune, by Boaz Gilad

Rental Houses for the Successful Small Investor, by Suzanne Thomas

Rich Dad, Poor Dad, by Robert Kiyosaki

The Unofficial Guide to Real Estate Investing, by Spencer Strauss and Martin Stone

What Every Real Estate Investor Needs to Know about Cash Flow, by Frank Galinelli

Appendix D
LETTERS AND FORMS

INTRODUCTION LETTER TO TENANTS AFTER PURCHASE OF NEW PROPERTY
Date
Dear tenant,
This letter is to inform you that I, (insert your name), have purchased (insert property address) and am the new owner of this building. I welcome all of you as tenants and look forward to getting to know each one of you.
Should you encounter a problem that needs to be addressed, please make me aware of the issue as soon as possible. Please contact me at the following address/phone number: (insert your phone number and PO Box. You could also provide your property manager's contact information).
Please be sure to mail all rent checks no later than the 1st of the month to the address listed above. Also, please be sure to make each check out to (your name, management company, or company name).
I look forward to working with all of you over the coming years.
Kind regards,
(Insert your name or property manager's name)

REQUEST FOR CRIME REPORT
FROM LOCAL POLICE STATION

Date

Attn: Police Officer at local station

From: (insert your name)

Could you provide me with a crime report and a "call to service" report for the following property address: (insert property address)

Thank you,

Landlord (Insert your name and contact information)

RENTAL APPLICATION

(SUBJECT TO LANDLORD'S APPROVAL)

SEPARATE APPLICATION REQUIRED
FROM EACH APPLICANT OVER AGE 18.

THIS SECTION TO BE COMPLETED BY LANDLORD

Address of Property to Be Rented:

Unit _____, _____, City, STATE, Zip Code

Rental Term: _____ month-to-month

_____ lease from _____ to _____

Amounts Due Before Occupancy:

First Month	Last Month	Security Deposit	TOTAL

THIS SECTION TO BE COMPLETED BY APPLICANT

Full Name (include all names used): _____

Date of Birth _____ / _____ / _____

Home Phone: ( ) _____

Work Phone: ( ) _____

Social Security Number: _____

Driver's License and State: _____

Vehicle Make: _____

Model: _____   Color: _____

Year: _____

License Plate Number & State: _____

Appendix D

Additional Occupants: *List everyone, including children, who will live with you in the apartment*

FULL NAME	to Applicant Relationship	Adult or Minor? if Minor, List Age
1)		
2)		
3)		
4)		

Rental History

Current Address: _____

City: _____ State: _____ Zip: _____

Dates Lived at Address: From _____ to _____

Reason for Leaving: _____

Landlord/Manager: _____

Phone: (   )_____

Previous Address: _____

City: _____ State: _____ Zip: _____

Dates Lived at Address: From _____ to _____

Reason for Leaving: _____

Landlord/Manager: _____

Phone: (   )_____

Letters and Forms

Employment History

Name of Current Employer: _____

Address: _____

Position or Title: _____

Phone: (   )_____

Name of Supervisor: _____

Supervisor's Phone: (   )_____

Dates Employed at This Job: From _____ to Present

Income

Current Monthly Salary	Average Monthly Other Income	Total Monthly Income

Financial Accounts

	Bank/Institution	Branch (City, State)
Savings Account		
Checking Account		
Other Financial Acct.		

Credit Accounts and Loans

	Type (Visa/Master/ student or car loan, etc.)	Name of Creditor	Amount Owed	Monthly Payment
Major credit card				
Major credit card				
Loan				
Other major obligations				

Appendix D

Miscellaneous

Describe the number and type of pets you want to have in the rental property: _____

Describe water-filled furniture you want to have in the rental property:

_____

Do you smoke? ____ Yes   ____ No

Have you ever:

Filed for bankruptcy?

Been sued?

Been evicted?

Been convicted of a crime?

Received *any* "notice to quit"?

Explain any "yes" in a separate sheet.

References and Emergency Contact

Personal Reference: _____

Relationship: _____

Address: _____

Phone: (   )_____

Personal Reference: _____

Relationship: _____

Address:_____

Phone: (   )_____

Emergency Contact: _____

Relationship: _____

Letters and Forms

Address: _____

Phone: (   )_____

I certify under pains and penalties of perjury that I am over the age of eighteen (18) and all the information given above is <u>true, complete, and correct</u>. _____ (Initials)

I understand that (1) my lease agreement may be terminated if I have made any false or incomplete statement in this application, (2) neither Landlord nor Landlord's agent(s) is responsible for the loss of personal belongings caused by fire, theft, smoke, water or otherwise, unless caused by their negligence; (3) base rent and other monthly charges are due and payable on the first day of each month in advance; (4) if applicable, deposit is to be applied as shown above, or applied to actual damages sustained by Landlord, except that it is to be refunded if this application is not accepted by Landlord; and (5) this application and, if any, deposits are taken subject to other applications and Landlord's approval, which approval is not effective unless in writing signed by Landlord. _____ (Initials)

I hereby authorize the release to an independent pre-rental screening agency of Landlord's choice (the "Agency") of any information held by any parties regarding my employment, criminal, credit, and information regarding my general character and reputation. I release any providers of such information from any liability for providing the information. I understand the information may be reviewed initially and periodically by the Agency and reported to my prospective Landlord. I further acknowledge that the Agency is relying on the third-party information, and I therefore release the Agency, my prospective Landlord, and their respective owners, officers, agents, and employees from any and all liability arising out of errors or omissions. _____ (Initials)

SIGNED: _____

DATE: _____

PRINT NAME: _____

STANDARD FORM APARTMENT LEASE
(FIXED TERM)

Date_____/_____/_____

_____

(Name of Lessor)

_____

(Address)   (Telephone No.)

Lessor, hereby leases to _____ _____

(Name)   (Address)

_____

(Telephone No.)

Lessee, who hereby hires the following premises: (Apartment) _____**#Uni**t located at

_____

(Street, City, State, and Zip code)

(consisting of) _____

(Unit description)

for the term of _____, beginning _____

and terminating on _____ The rent to be paid by the Lessee for the leased premises shall be as follows:

RENT and Security Deposit   **A:** The term rent shall be **ANNUAL**, payable, except as herein otherwise provided, in installments of $_____ **MONTHLY**, on the Last day of every month, in advance, so long as this lease is in force and effect; and a Security Deposit of $_____, for a total payment of $_____. All payments are to be made payable to [INSERT YOUR NAME OR COMPANY].

SECURITY DEPOSITS: The total of the above deposits shall secure compliance with the terms and conditions of this agreement and shall be refunded to RESIDENT within 30 days after the premises have been completely vacated less any amount necessary to pay OWNER: (a) any unpaid rent, (b) cleaning costs, (c) key replacement costs, (d) cost for repair of damages to premises and/or common areas above ordinary wear and tear, and (e) any other amount legally allowable under the terms of this agreement. A written accounting of said charges shall be presented to RESIDENT within 30 days of move-out. If deposits do not cover such costs and damages, the RESIDENT shall immediately pay said additional costs for damages to OWNER.

LESSOR AND LESSEE FURTHER COVENANT AND AGREE:

1. MAINTENANCE — For maintenance, if other than lessor, contact:

(Name)   (Address)   (Telephone No.)

2. SMOKING   Smoking shall not be permitted in the Leased Premises.

Letters and Forms

3. HEAT AND OTHER UTILITIES

The Lessee shall pay, as they become due, all bills for electricity and other utilities, whether they are used for furnishing heat or other purposes, that are furnished to the demised premises and separately metered.

TENANT: This section governs utility payments. Be sure to discuss with the Lessor those payments that will be required of you for this apartment.

4. ATTACHED FORMS

The forms, if any, attached hereto are incorporated herein by reference.

5. CARE OF PREMISES

The Lessee shall not paint, decorate, or otherwise embellish and/or change and shall not make nor suffer any additions or alterations to be made in or to the leased premises without the prior written consent of the Lessor, nor make nor suffer any strip or waste, nor suffer the heat or water to be wasted, and at the termination of this lease shall deliver up the leased premises and all property belonging to the Lessor in good, clean, and tenantable order and condition, reasonable wear and tear excepted. No washing machine, air-conditioning unit, space heater, clothes dryer, or other aerials, or other like equipment shall be installed without the prior written consent of the Lessor. No waterbeds shall be permitted in the leased premises.

6. CLEANLINESS

The Lessee shall maintain the leased premises in a clean condition. He shall not sweep, throw, or dispose of, nor permit to be swept, thrown, or disposed of, from said premises or from any doors, windows, balconies, porches, or other parts of said building, any dirt, waste, rubbish, or other substance or article into any other parts of said building or the land adjacent thereon, except in proper receptacles and except in accordance with the rules of the Lessor.

7. DEFINITIONS

The words "Lessor" and "Lessee" as used herein shall include their respective heirs, executors, administrators, successors, representatives and assigns, agents, and servants; and the words "he", "his," and "him" where applicable shall apply to the Lessor or Lessee regardless of sex, number, corporate entity, trust, or other body. If more than one party signs as Lessee hereunder, the covenants, conditions, and agreements herein of the Lessee shall be the joint and several obligations of each such party.

8. DELIVERY OF PREMISES

In the event the Lessor is not able through no fault of his own to deliver the leased premises to the Lessee at the time called for herein, the rent shall be abated on a pro rata basis until such time as occupancy can be obtained, which abatement shall constitute full settlement of all damages caused by such delay, or the Lessor, at his election, shall be allowed reasonable time to deliver possession of the leased premises, and if he cannot deliver such possession within 30 days from the beginning of said term, either the Lessor or Lessee may then terminate this lease by giving written notice to the other and any payment made under this lease shall be forthwith refunded. Lessee hereby authorizes and empowers Lessor to institute proceedings to recover possession of the premises on behalf of and in the name of Lessee.

9. EMINENT DOMAIN

If the leased premises, or any part thereof, or the whole or any part of the building of which they are a part, shall be taken for any purpose by exercise of the power of eminent domain or condemnation, or by action of the city or other authorities, or shall receive any direct or consequential damage for which the Lessor or Lessee shall be entitled to compensation by reason of anything lawfully done in pursuance of any public authority after the execution hereof and during said term, or any extension or renewal thereof, then at the option of either the Lessor or the Lessee, this lease and said term shall terminate and

Appendix D

such option may be exercised in the case of any such taking, notwithstanding the entire interest of the Lessor and the Lessee may have been divested by such taking. Said option to terminate shall be exercised by either the Lessor or the Lessee, by giving a written notice of exercise of such option to terminate in the manner described in Section 17 of this lease. Said option to terminate shall not be exercised by either party (a) earlier than the effective date of taking, nor (b) later than thirty (30) days after the effective date of taking. The mailing of the notice of exercise as set forth hereinabove shall be deemed to be the exercise of said option; and upon the giving of such notice, this lease shall be terminated as of the date of the taking. If this lease and said term are not so terminated, then in case of any such taking or destruction of or damage to the leased premises, rendering the same or any part thereof unfit for use and occupation, a just proportion of the rent hereinbefore reserved, according to the nature and extent of the damage to the leased premises, shall be suspended or abated until, in the case of such taking, what may remain of the leased premises shall have been put in proper condition for use and occupation. The Lessee hereby assigns to the Lessor any and all claims and demands for damages on account of any such taking or for compensation for anything lawfully done in pursuance of any public authority, and covenants with the Lessor that the Lessee will from time to time execute and deliver to the Lessor such further instruments of assignment of any such claims and demands as the Lessor shall request, provided however that the Lessee does not assign to the Lessor any claims based upon Lessee's personal property or other improvements installed by Lessee with Lessor's written permission.

10. FIRE, OTHER CASUALTY

If the leased premises, or any part thereof, or the whole or a substantial part of the building of which they are a part, shall be destroyed or damaged by fire or other casualty after the execution hereof and during said term, or any extension or renewal thereof, then this lease and said term shall terminate at the option of the Lessor by notice to the Lessee. If this lease and said term are not so terminated, then in case of any such destruction of or damage to the leased premises, or to the common areas of the building customarily used by the Lessee for access to and egress from the leased premises, rendering the same or any part thereof unfit for use and occupation, a just proportion of the rent hereinbefore reserved, according to the nature and extent of the damage to the leased premises, shall be suspended or abated until the leased premises shall have been put in proper condition for use and occupation. If the leased premises or such common areas have not been restored by the Lessor to substantially their former condition for use and occupancy within thirty (30) days after the damage occurred, the Lessee may terminate this lease by giving notice to the Lessor within thirty days following the termination of the thirty-day period within which the Lessor failed to restore. If either party gives notice of intention to terminate under this section, this lease shall terminate on the last day of the then-current monthly rental period.

11. DISTURBANCE, ILLEGAL USE

Neither the Lessee nor his family, friends, relatives, invitees, visitors, agents, or servants shall make or suffer any unlawful, noisy, or otherwise offensive use of the leased premises, nor commit or permit any nuisance to exist thereon, nor cause damage to the leased premises, nor create any substantial interference with the rights, comfort, safety, or enjoyment of the Lessor or other occupants of the same or any other apartment, nor make any use whatsoever thereof than as and for a private residence. No articles shall be hung or shaken from the windows, doors, porches, or balconies, or placed upon the exterior windowsills.

12. GOVERNMENTAL REGULATIONS

The Lessor shall be obligated to fulfill all of the Lessor's obligations hereunder to the best of the Lessor's ability, but the Lessee's obligations, covenants, and agreements hereunder shall not (subject to applicable law) be affected, impaired,

Letters and Forms

or excused because the Lessor is unable to supply or is delayed in supplying any service or is unable to make or is delayed in making any repairs, additions, alterations, or decorations, or is unable to supply or is delayed in supplying any equipment or fixtures, if Lessor is prevented or delayed from doing so because of any law or governmental action or any order, rule, or regulation of any governmental agency which is beyond the Lessor's reasonable control.

13. COMMON AREAS

No receptacles, vehicles, baby carriages, or other articles or obstructions shall be placed in the halls or other common areas or passageways.

14. INSURANCE

Lessee understands and agrees that it shall be Lessee's own obligation to insure his personal property.

15. KEYS AND LOCKS

Upon expiration or termination of the lease, the Lessee shall deliver the keys of the premises to the landlord. Delivery of keys by the Lessee to the Lessor, or to anyone on his behalf, shall not constitute a surrender or acceptance of surrender of the leased premises unless so stipulated in writing by the Lessor. In the event that the exterior door lock or locks in the leased premises are not in normal working order at any time during the term thereof, and if the Lessee reports such condition to the Lessor, then and in that event the Lessor shall, within a reasonable period of time following receipt of notice from the Lessee of such condition, repair or replace such lock or locks. Locks shall not be changed, altered, or replaced nor shall new locks be added by the Lessee without the written permission of the Lessor. Any locks so permitted to be installed shall become the property of the Lessor and shall not be removed by the Lessee. The Lessee shall promptly give a duplicated key to any such changed, altered, replaced, or new lock to the Lessor. If the Lessee loses their key(s), the Lessee is responsible for the costs to change the locks.

KEYS: In the event the LESSEE/TENANTS get locked out of the premises, the LESSEE/TENANTS agree to pay for the cost of the labor and materials to re-key the lock by a professional locksmith.

16. LOSS OR DAMAGE

The Lessee agrees to indemnify and save the Lessor harmless from all liability, loss, or damage arising from any nuisance made or suffered on the leased premises by the Lessee, his family, friends, relatives, invitees, visitors, agents, or servants or from any carelessness, neglect, or improper conduct of any such persons. All personal property in any part of the building within the control of the Lessee shall be at the sole risk of the Lessee. Subject to provisions of applicable law, the Lessor shall not be liable for damage to or loss of property of any kind which may be lost or stolen, damaged or destroyed by fire, water, steam, defective refrigeration, elevators, or otherwise, while on the leased premises or in any storage space in the building or for any personal injury unless caused by the negligence of the Lessor.

17. NOTICES

Written notice from the Lessor to the Lessee shall be deemed to have been properly given if mailed by registered or certified mail postage prepaid, return receipt requested to the Lessee at the address of the leased premises, or if delivered or left in or on any part thereof, provided that if so mailed, the receipt has been signed, or if so delivered or left, that such notice has been delivered to or left with the Lessee or anyone expressly or impliedly authorized to receive messages for the Lessee, or by any adult who resides with the Lessee in the leased premises. Written notice from the Lessee to the Lessor shall be deemed to have been properly given if mailed by registered or certified mail, postage prepaid, return receipt requested to the Lessor at his address set forth in the first paragraph of this lease, unless the Lessor shall have notified the Lessee of a change of the Lessor's address, in which case such notice shall be so sent to such changed address of the Lessor, provided that the receipt has been signed by the Lessor or anyone expressly or impliedly authorized to receive messages for the Lessor. *Notwithstanding the foregoing, notice by either party to the other shall be deemed adequate if given in any other manner authorized by law.*

18. OTHER REGULATIONS

The Lessee agrees to conform to such lawful rules and regulations which are reasonably related to the purpose and provisions of this lease, as shall from time to time be established by the Lessor in the future for the safety, care, cleanliness, or orderly conduct of the leased premises and the building of which they are a part, and of the benefit, safety, comfort, and convenience of all the occupants of said building.

19. PARKING

Parking on the premises of the Lessor is prohibited unless written consent is given by the Lessor.

20. PETS

No dogs or other animals, birds, or pets shall be kept in or upon the leased premises without the Lessor's written consent, and consent so given may be revoked at any time.

21. PLUMBING

The water closets, disposals, and waste pipes shall not be used for any purposes other than those for which they were constructed, nor shall any sweepings, rubbish, rags, or any other improper articles be thrown into same, and any damage to the building caused by the misuse of such equipment shall be borne by the Lessee by whom or upon whose premises shall have been caused unless caused by the negligence of the Lessor, or by the negligence of an independent contractor employed by the Lessor.

22. REPAIRS

The Lessee agrees with the Lessor that, during this lease and for such further time as the Lessee shall hold the leased premises or any part thereof, the Lessee will at all times keep and maintain the leased premises and all equipment and fixtures therein or used therewith repaired, whole, and of the same kind, quality, and description and in such good repair, order, and condition as the same are at the beginning of, or may be put in during the term or any extension or renewal thereof, reasonable wear and tear and damage by unavoidable casualty only excepted. The Lessor and the Lessee agree to comply with any responsibility that either may have under applicable law to perform repairs upon the leased premises. If Lessee fails within a reasonable time, or improperly makes such repairs, then and in any such event or events, the Lessor may (but shall not be obligated to) make such repairs and the Lessee shall reimburse the Lessor for the reasonable cost of such repairs in full, upon demand.

23. RIGHT OF ENTRY

The Lessor may enter upon the leased premises to make repairs thereto, to inspect the premises, or to show the premises to prospective tenants, purchasers, or mortgagees. The Lessor may also enter upon the said premises if same appear to have been abandoned by the Lessee or as otherwise permitted by law.

24. NONPERFORMANCE OR BREACH BY LESSEE

If the Lessee shall fail to comply with any lawful term, condition, covenant, obligation, or agreement expressed herein or implied hereunder, or if the Lessee shall be declared bankrupt, or insolvent according to law, or if any assignment of the Lessee's property shall be made for the benefit of creditors, or if the premises appear to be abandoned, then, and in any of the said cases and notwithstanding any license or waiver of any prior breach of any of the said terms, conditions, covenants, obligations, or agreements the Lessor, without necessity or requirement of making any entry, may (subject to the Lessee's rights under applicable law) terminate this lease by:

   1. a seven (7) day written notice to the Lessee to vacate said leased premises in case of any breach except only for nonpayment of rent, or

2. a fourteen (14) day written notice to the Lessee to vacate said leased premises upon the neglect or refusal of the Lessee to pay the rent as herein provided.

Any termination under this section shall be without prejudice to any remedies which might otherwise be used for arrears of rent or preceding breach of any of the said terms, conditions, covenants, obligations, or agreements.

25. LESSEE'S COVENANTS IN EVENT OF TERMINATION

The Lessee covenants that in case of any termination of this lease, by reason of the default of the Lessee, then at the option of Lessor:

(A) the Lessee will forthwith pay to the Lessor as damages hereunder a sum equal to the amount by which the rent and other payments called for hereunder for the remainder of the term or any extension or renewal thereof exceed the fair rental value of said premises for the remainder of the term or any extension or renewal thereof; and

(B) the Lessee covenants that he will furthermore indemnify the Lessor from and against any loss and damage sustained by reason of any termination caused by the default of, or the breach by, the Lessee. Lessor's damages hereunder shall include, but shall not be limited to, any loss of rents; reasonable broker's commissions for the re-letting of the leased premises; advertising costs; the reasonable cost incurred in cleaning and repainting the premises in order to re-let the same; and moving and storage charges incurred by Lessor in moving Lessee's belongings pursuant to eviction proceedings.

(C) At the option of the Lessor, however, Lessor's cause of action under this article shall accrue when a new tenancy or lease term first commences subsequent to a termination under this lease, in which event Lessor's damages shall be limited to any and all damages sustained by him prior to said new tenancy or lease date.

Lessor shall also be entitled to any and all other remedies provided by law. All rights and remedies are to be cumulative and not exclusive.

26. REMOVAL OF GOODS

Lessee further covenants and agrees that if Lessor shall remove Lessee's goods or effects, pursuant to the terms hereof or of any Court order, Lessor shall not be liable or responsible for any loss of or damage to Lessee's goods or effects and the Lessor's act of so removing such goods or effects shall be deemed to be the act of and for the account of Lessee, provided, however, that if the Lessor removes the Lessee's goods or effects, he shall comply with all applicable laws, and shall exercise due care in the handling of such goods to the fullest practical extent under the circumstances.

27. NONSURRENDER

Neither the vacating of the premises by the Lessee, nor the delivery of keys to the Lessor shall be deemed a surrender or an acceptance of surrender of the leased premises, unless so stipulated in writing by Lessor.

28. SUBLETTING, NUMBER OF OCCUPANTS

The Lessee shall not assign nor underlet any part or the whole of the leased premises, nor shall permit the leased premises to be occupied for a period longer than a temporary visit by anyone *except the individuals specifically named in the first paragraph of this lease*, their spouses, and any children born to them during the term of this lease or any extension or renewal thereof without first obtaining on each occasion the assent in writing of the Lessor.

29. TRUSTEE

In the event that the Lessor is a trustee or a partnership, no such trustee nor any beneficiary nor any shareholder of said trust and no partner, General or Limited, of such partnership shall be personally liable to anyone under any term, condition, covenant, obligation, or agreement expressed herein or implied hereunder or for any claim of damage or cause at law or in equity arising out of the occupancy of said leased premises, the use or the maintenance of said building or its approaches or equipment.

30. WAIVER

The waiver of one breach of any term, condition, covenant, obligation, or agreement of this lease shall not be considered to be a waiver of that or any other term, condition, covenant, obligation, or agreement or of any subsequent breach thereof.

31. SEPARABILITY CLAUSE

If any provision of this lease or portion of such provision or the application thereof to any person or circumstance is held invalid, the remainder of the lease (or the remainder of such provision) and the application thereof to other persons or circumstances shall not be affected thereby.

32. REPRISALS PROHIBITED

The Lessor acknowledges that provisions of applicable law forbid a landlord from threatening to take or taking reprisals against any tenant for seeking to assert his legal rights.

33. OTHER PROVISIONS

LIQUID-FILLED FURNISHINGS: No liquid-filled furniture, receptacle containing more than ten gallons of liquid is permitted without prior written consent and meeting the requirements of the OWNER. RESIDENT also agrees to carry insurance deemed appropriate by OWNER to cover possible losses that may be caused by such items.

NOISE: RESIDENT agrees not to cause or allow any noise or activity on the premises that might disturb the peace and quiet of another RESIDENT and/or neighbor. Said noise and/or activity shall be a breach of this agreement.

DESTRUCTION OF PREMISES: If the premises become totally or partially destroyed during the term of this Agreement so that RESIDENT'S use is seriously impaired, OWNER or RESIDENT may terminate this Agreement immediately upon three-day written notice to the other.

SATELLITE TV DISH: These may not be attached to the roof of the building in any fashion. These must be mounted to the side of the property or on a pole in the yard. Resident agrees to a $200 fine if dish is attached to the roof of building.

IN WITNESS WHEREOF, the said parties hereunto and to another instrument of like tenor, have set their hands and seals on the day and year first above written; and Lessee as an individual states under the pains and penalties of perjury that said Lessee is over the age of 18 years.

_____
Lessee

_____
Lessor

_____

_____
Trustee or Agent

Disclosure of Information on Lead-Based Paint and/or Lead-Based Paint Hazards

Lead Warning Statement

Housing built before 1978 may contain lead-based paint. Lead from paint, paint chips, and dust can pose health hazards if not managed properly. Lead exposure is especially harmful to young children and pregnant women. Before renting pre-1978 housing, lessors must disclose the presence of known lead-based paint and/or lead-based paint hazards in the dwelling. Lessees must also receive a federally approved pamphlet on lead poisoning prevention.

Lessor's Disclosure

Presence of lead-based paint and/or lead-based paint hazards (check (i) or (ii) below):

(i) Known lead-based paint and/or lead-based paint hazards are present in the housing (explain).

_____

(ii) Lessor has no knowledge of lead-based paint and/or lead-based paint hazards in the housing.

Records and reports available to the lessor (check (i) or (ii) below):

(i) Lessor has provided the lessee with all available records and reports pertaining to lead-based paint and/or lead-based paint hazards in the housing (list documents below)

_____

(ii) Lessor has no reports or records pertaining to lead-based paint and/or lead-based paint hazards in the housing.

Lessee's Acknowledgment (initial)

_____ Lessee has received copies of all information listed above.

_____ Lessee has received the pamphlet *Protect Your Family from Lead in Your Home.*

Agent's Acknowledgment (initial)

_____ Agent has informed the lessor of the lessor's obligations under 42 U.S.C. 4852(d) and is aware of his/her responsibility to ensure compliance.

Certification of Accuracy

The following parties have reviewed the information above and certify, to the best of their knowledge, that the information they have provided is true and accurate.

_____

Lessor

_____

Lessee

Tenant Certification Form
Required Federal Lead Warning Statement

Housing built before 1978 may contain lead-based paint. Lead from paint, paint chips, and dust can pose health hazards if not managed properly. Lead exposure is especially harmful to young children and pregnant women. Before renting pre-1978 housing, lessors must disclose the presence of known lead-based paint and/or lead-based paint hazards in the dwelling. Lessees must also receive a federally approved pamphlet on lead poisoning prevention. The Massachusetts Tenant Lead Law Notification and Certification Form is for compliance with state and federal lead notification requirements.

Owner's Disclosure

(a) Presence of lead-based paint and/or lead-based paint hazards (check (i) or (ii) below):

(i) _____Known lead-based paint and/or lead-based paint hazards are present in the housing (explain).

_____

(ii) _____Owner/Lessor has no knowledge of lead-based paint and/or lead-based paint hazards in the housing.

(b) Records and reports available to the owner/lessor (check (i) or (ii) below):

(i) _____Owner/Lessor has provided the tenant with all available records and reports pertaining to lead-based paint and/or lead-based paint hazards in the housing (circle documents below).

Lead Inspection Report; Risk Assessment Report; Letter of Interim Control; Letter of Compliance

(ii) _____Owner/Lessor has no reports or records pertaining to lead-based paint and/or lead-based paint hazards in the housing.

Tenant's Acknowledgment (initial)

(c) _____Tenant has received copies of all documents circled above.

(d) _____Tenant has received no documents listed above.

(e) _____Tenant has received the Massachusetts Tenant Lead Law Notification.

Agent's Acknowledgment (initial)

(f) _____Agent has informed the owner/lessor of the owner's/lessor's obligations under federal and state law for lead-based paint disclosure and notification and is aware of his/her responsibility to ensure compliance.

Certification of Accuracy

The following parties have reviewed the information above and certify, to the best of their knowledge, that the information they have provided is true and accurate.

_____   _____
Owner/Lessor   Date   Owner/Lessor   Date

Letters and Forms

Tenant	Date	Tenant	Date

Agent	Date	Agent	Date

Owner/Managing Agent Information for Tenant (Please Print):

Name Street Apt.

_____

City/Town   Zip   Telephone

_____I (owner/managing agent) certify that I provided the Tenant Lead Law Notification/ Tenant Certification Form and any existing Lead Law documents to the tenant, but the tenant refused to sign this certification.

The tenant gave the following reason: _____

_____

The Lead Law prohibits rental discrimination, including refusing to rent to families with children or evicting families with children because of lead paint.

Contact the Childhood Lead Poisoning Prevention Program for information on the availability of this form in other languages.

Tenant and owner must each keep a completed and signed copy of this form.

Apartment Condition Statement

Street Address:	
Unit #	
Tenant	

This form shall serve as a statement as to the condition of the above premises, when rented to the tenant on the date that this statement was signed. The tenant agrees to the condition of the apartment, and agrees to maintain the apartment in good condition throughout the terms in the lease. Any additional improvements to said apartment may be performed at specified time intervals when agreed upon by both the tenant and the landlord.

CONDITION OF PREMISES: RESIDENT acknowledges that he has examined the premises and that said premises, all furnishings, fixtures, furniture, plumbing, heating, electrical facilities, all other items listed on this attachment, if any, and/or all other items provided by OWNER are all clean, and in good satisfactory condition except as may be indicated elsewhere in this Agreement. LESSEE agrees to keep the premises and all items in good order and good condition and to immediately pay for costs to repair and/or replace any portion of the above damaged by LESSEE, his guests and/or invitees, except as provided by law. At the termination of this Agreement, all of the above items in this provision shall be returned to LESSOR in clean and good condition except for reasonable wear and tear and the premises shall be free of all personal property and trash not belonging to LESSOR. It is agreed that all dirt, holes, tears, burns, and stains of any size or amount in the carpets, drapes, walls, fixtures, and/or any other part of the premises, do not constitute reasonable wear and tear.

This apartment has the following defects:

_____

_____

_____

_____

Landlord:	Date:
Tenant:	Date:

Mold Addendum

1. LEASE CONTRACT DESCRIPTION.

Residential Lease date: _____,

Landlord or agent's name:

Tenants (list all residents):

The Residential Lease is referred to in this Mold Addendum as the "Lease Contract."

2. **MOLD AND MILDEW.** You acknowledge that it is necessary for you to maintain appropriate climate control, keep your dwelling unit clean, and take necessary measures to retard and prevent mold from accumulating in the dwelling unit. You agree to clean and dust the dwelling unit on a regular basis and to remove visible moisture accumulation on windows, windowsills, walls, floors, ceilings, and other surfaces as soon as reasonably possible. You agree not to block or cover any heating, ventilation, or air-conditioning ducts. You also agree to report immediately in writing to us: (i) any evidence of a water leak or excessive moisture in the dwelling unit, common hallways, storage room, garage, or other common area; (ii) any evidence of mold that cannot be removed with a common household cleaner; (iii) any failure or malfunction in heating, ventilation, or air conditioning, and (iv) any inoperable doors or windows. You further agree that you shall be responsible for damage to the dwelling unit and your personal property as well as any injury to you and all occupants of the dwelling unit resulting from your failure to comply with the terms of this Mold Addendum.

3. **VIOLATION OF RULES.** If you or any occupant violates any rule or provision of this Mold Addendum (based upon our judgment) it shall be considered a material default under the terms of the Lease Contract. Upon written notice from us, you must immediately comply with all rules and provisions of this Mold Addendum. We also have all other rights and remedies set forth in the Lease Contract, including damages, eviction, and attorneys' fees to the extent allowed by law.

4. **LIABILITY FOR DAMAGES, INJURIES, CLEANING, ETC.** You and all tenants under the Lease contract are fully responsible and liable for the entire amount of all cleaning expenses incurred by us to remove mold from the dwelling unit as well as all damages to the dwelling unit caused by mold. We—not you—will arrange for these services. If a part or parts of the dwelling unit cannot be satisfactorily cleaned or repaired, you must pay for us to replace them completely. Payments for damages, repairs, cleaning, replacements, etc., are due immediately upon demand.

5. **GENERAL.** This Mold Addendum is considered part of the Lease Contract described above. In the event of any conflict between the terms of this Mold Addendum and the terms of the Lease Contract, the terms of this Mold Addendum shall control.

Each tenant who signed the Lease Contract must sign this Mold Addendum. Each tenant is jointly and severally liable for damages and all other obligations set forth in this Mold Addendum.

This Mold Addendum is a legally binding contract. Read it carefully before signing.

You are entitled to receive an original of this Mold Addendum after it is fully signed. Keep it in a safe place.

Date

Tenants _____

_____

Date

Landlord or Agent _____

Please note: In this document, the terms "you" and "your" refer to all tenants listed above and all occupants or guests; and the terms "we," "us," and "our" refer to the landlord or agent named in the Lease Contract (not to the property manager or anyone else). In this document, all references to the term "mold" shall be deemed to include all forms of mold and mildew as well as similar growths.

Notice to Terminate Tenancy

To: _____

And all other tenants in possession of the premises listed above.

Address:

_____

Street, Unit #, City, State, Zip Code

TAKE NOTICE that you are hereby required within ____ days to remove from and deliver up possession of the above-described premises that you currently hold and occupy. The notice is intended for the purposes of terminating the Rental Agreement by which you now hold possession of the above-described premises, and should you fail to comply, legal proceedings will commence to regain possession. **FAILURE TO RESPOND TO THIS NOTICE SHALL RESULT IN DUE PROCESS OF LAW FOR EVICTION AND COLLECTION OF AMOUNTS DUE TO BE COMMENCED AND FOR OTHER REMEDIES AVAILABLE TO LANDLORD FOR WHICH YOU WILL BE RESPONSIBLE FOR COSTS AND ATTORNEY FEES.**

_____

Landlord/Owner

_____

Date

On _____, this notice was delivered to the tenant(s)

Executed on _____, at the City of _____, County of

_____, State of _____, Served by: _____

Notice to Pay Rent or Quit

To: _____

And all other tenants in possession of the premises listed above.

Address:

_____

Street, Unit #, City, State, Zip Code

TAKE NOTICE that rent is now due and payable on the above-described premises that you currently occupy. Your rent is delinquent in the amount listed below:

Rental period: _____	Rent Due: $_____
Rental period: _____	Rent Due: $_____
Rental period: _____	Rent Due: $_____
Rental period: _____	Rent Due: $_____
	Total due: $_____

You are hereby required to pay the total amount due within ___ days or to remove from and deliver up possession of the premises, or legal action will be taken against you to recover rents, damages, court costs, and attorney's fees, according to your Lease agreement.

_____

Landlord/Owner

_____

Date

On _____, this notice was delivered to the tenant(s)

Executed on _____, at the City of _____, County of

_____, State of _____, Served by: _____

Index

Index

Bankruptcy, 38, 87
Banks:
    developing relationship with, 75
    as key team members, 156–157
    largest commercial lenders, 70–71
    as source of down payment, 71–72
    as source of motivated sellers, 46
Better Business Bureau (BBB), 147
Birthday cards, for tenants, 102
Bonuses, for contractors, 147
Business plans, 17, 178

Cable television, 139
Capital expenditures, reserves for,
    175, 179
Capital gains taxes, 8, 163–164, 165
Capitalization approach (*see* Income
    [capitalization] approach)
Capitalization rate (cap rate), 50–51,
    54, 55, 57, 58, 142, 160, 161,
    172
Carpenters, 155–156
Cash flow, 8–10, 106
    break-even, 59–60
    from condominiums, 11–13
    defined, 8
    financing and, 76–77
    freedom and, 9–10, 181–182
    negative, 11–12, 54, 172
    positive before-tax, 8, 59, 76–77,
    179
    reliability of, 9
Cash-on-cash return, 7, 57, 58
Cash-out refinancing, 5, 18, 72–73
Children, 101
    de-lead certification and, 30–31,
    116–117
    discrimination against families
    with, 32, 117
    fire emergencies and, 141
Closing process, 79–81, 175
Cockroaches, 122
Commissions:
    deposits and, 78

Commissions (*Cont.*):
    real estate broker, 17–18, 38–39,
    42–43, 45, 78, 177
    from title companies, 65
Commitment letters, 78, 80
Comparable sales approach, 50
Competition:
    apartment qualities and amenities,
    81
    in finding deals, 35, 82
    in finding tenants, 93–94, 98
    of real estate brokers, 156
    in real estate investing, 169–180
Condominiums, 11–14
    appreciation of, 12–13
    conversion projects, 22, 160, 161,
    170–174
    as residence versus income
    properties, 11–12, 165–166
Constables, 46, 125–128
Construction loans, 141
Construction materials, 148, 149
Contingencies, 22, 77–78, 117
Contractors, 145–152, 155–156, 177
Contracts, with vendors, 143, 147,
    148–149
Craigslist.org, 35, 44–45
Credit cards, 73, 149–150
Credit reports, 70, 87, 98, 115–116
Credit scores, 75–76, 87, 115
Credit unions, as source of down
    payment, 71–72
Curb appeal, 94

Damages to property, 110, 116, 119,
    140, 141, 150–151
DCR (debt coverage ratio), 58, 59
De-lead certification, 30–31, 116–117
Deal evaluation, 49–61
    break even in, 59–60
    comparable sales approach, 50
    income (capitalization) approach,
    50–59
    replacement cost approach, 50

Index

Index

Index

Interest expense deduction, 72
Interest-only programs, 66–69
Interest rates:
    adjustable, 64, 66–70
    annual interest rate, 64
    fixed, 64, 65–69
    net operating income (NOI) and,
       160
    starter, 69
Intermediaries, in 1031 tax
    exchanges, 163, 164–165
Internal rate of return (IRR), 57
Internet (*see* Online information)

Job growth trends, 160

Keys, 81, 137
Kickbacks, 146
Kitchens, requirements for, 124
Knocking on doors, to find sellers of
    property, 40

Landlord and investor clubs, 26, 38,
    40–41, 45, 157–158
Landlords:
    property managers versus, 104,
       114, 131
    real estate investors versus,
       132–133
    reference checks with, 97, 115
    visiting of property by, 136, 174
Landscaping services, 99–100, 143
Lawyers (*see* Attorneys; Legal issues)
Lead paint, 30–31, 116–117
Leases, 96–97, 120, 140
Legal issues, 113–130
    (see also specific legal issues)
Lenders (*see* Banks)
Leverage, 5, 6–7, 166, 169
Lightbulbs, 138
Like-kind property, in 1031 tax
    exchanges, 162–165
Liquidation strategy (*see* Exit strategy)
Listing agents, 17–18, 43

LLC (limited liability company), 83
Local publications, advertising vacan-
    cies in, 90
Location, in finding deals, 29, 34, 132
Lockboxes, 105
Locks, 123, 137
LoopNet, 44, 45, 174
Low-document-verification loan
    approvals, 71–72, 74–75
Low-flow fixtures, 136
Low-income families (*see* Section 8
    tenants)
LTV (loan to value), for home equity
    loans, 72

Mailing lists, to find sellers of prop-
    erty, 40
Master key systems, 137
Materials lists, 149
Mediation, for evictions, 127–128
Mentors, importance of, 13, 29, 157,
    174
Military tenants, 93
Mixed-used properties, 173–174
MLS (Multiple Listing Service), 17,
    42–45, 174
Mortgage applications, 80
Mortgage brokers, 17, 63–64,
    156–157
Mortgage programs, 65–71
    adjustable, 64, 66–70
    fixed, 64, 65–69
    information sources for, 70
    interest-only, 66–69
    largest commercial lenders, 70–71
Motivated sellers:
    finding, 37–46
    making offers to, 22–23, 30
Move-in/out, 116, 128–129
Multiunit properties, 12, 33–34, 44

National Association of Home
    Builders, 81
National Association of Realtors, 44

223

Index

Index

Rapport, establishing, 93
Real estate brokers:
  commissions of, 17–18, 38–39,
    42–43, 45, 78, 177
  contact lists, 17–18, 42–43
  finder's fee and, 43–44, 115
  finding experienced, 16
  as key team members, 156
  listing agents, 17–18, 43
  pocket listings, 17–18, 42–43
  as source of motivated sellers,
    42–43
  training for, 133, 177
Real estate investing:
  advantages of, 3–10
  appreciation in, 5–6
  cash flow from, 8–10
  characteristics of successful
    investors, 176–179
  competition in, 169–180
  examples of, 15–32
  landlord and investor clubs, 26, 38,
    40–41, 45, 157–158
  landlords versus, 132–133
  leverage from, 5, 6–7, 166, 169
  steps to success in, 174–176
  strategy for, 15–16, 29
  (See also Tax savings)
Realtor-com, 44
Reasonable accommodation,
  121–122
Receipts:
  for advance payments, 118
  for property expenses, 135
Receivership properties, 29–30
Record keeping, 105–107, 114,
  117–118, 175
Reference checks, 96–97, 111, 115,
  146, 147
Referral fees, for new tenants, 92
Refinancing, cash-out, 5, 18,
  72–73
Refrigerators, 124
REITs, 171

Relinquished property, in 1031 tax
  exchanges, 160, 162–165
Renovations, 19, 21–22, 30, 36–37,
  166, 170, 176, 177
Rent levels:
  FMR (fair market rent), 107, 108,
    110, 111
  knowledge of local market and,
    100–101
  rent increases, 121
  tenant retention and, 101–104
Rent payments:
  Notice to Quit eviction, 126
  timely receipt of, 105
Rental income:
  collection methods, 105
  record keeping and, 105–107
  reporting, 107
  (See also Revenue)
Repairs:
  handling, 102, 103–104, 123–124,
    150
  records of, 106
  reserves for, 175, 179
Replacement cost approach, 50
Replacement property, in 1031 tax
  exchanges, 160, 162–165
Reserves, importance of, 175, 179
Retirement accounts, 4, 73
Revenue:
  ancillary, sources of, 144
  in income (capitalization) approach,
    50, 52, 53, 56, 142–144
  (See also Rental income)
Rodents, 101, 122

Safety, in finding deals, 34–35
Sales of property (see Exit strategy)
Satellite television, 139–140
Savings:
  inflation and, 4
  as source of down payment, 73
Screening applicants, 95–97, 111,
  115–116, 141–142, 175

Index

About the Author

Matthew Martinez spent a decade working in the high-tech industry before discovering real estate as a profession. After receiving his B.S.B.A. and master's degree in international studies, he worked at the U.S. Embassy in London and was a member of the White House Advance Team during the Clinton administration's second term. He has also lived and worked in Italy, Mexico, Australia, Singapore, and several countries throughout South America. In 1999, he moved to New England to work for one of the early Internet search engine firms and purchased his first home in Boston. Shortly thereafter, he began acquiring rental properties. From 2002 through 2004, he purchased several million dollars worth of income-producing properties and founded the Landlord and Investor Group, an organization with more than 700 members that helps investors excel in the real estate industry by educating and sharing best practices and time-proven strategies. By 2004, Martinez was able to leave his corporate job and dedicate all of his time to real estate endeavors. He is now the principal of Pangea Select, a real estate investment company that acquires multi-family properties in emerging, high-growth areas throughout the United States.

Author's e-mail: matt@landlordandinvestor.com

The Landlord and Investor Group: www.landlordandinvestor.com (to subscribe to the real estate newsletter)

Pangea Select: www.pangeaselect.com (to learn about specific investment opportunities)